WHAT CHILD IS THIS?

WHAT CHILD IS THIS?

WITNESSES TO THE BIRTH OF CHRIST

RUBEL SHELLY

HOWARD
PUBLISHING CO.

3117 North 7th
West Monroe, Louisiana 71291

Our purpose at Howard Publishing is:

• **Inspiring** holiness in the lives of believers,

• **Instilling** hope in the hearts of struggling people everywhere,

• **Instructing** believers toward a deeper faith in Jesus Christ,

Because he's coming again.

Published by Howard Publishing Co., Inc.
3117 North 7th Street, West Monroe, LA 71291-2227

Printed in the United States of America

First Printing

Cover Design by Steve Diggs & Friends

ISBN# 1-878990-23-3

CONTENTS

INTRODUCTION

So many special things are associated with the birth of a baby. Any baby.

Suspense and anxiety, excitement and planning, picking a name and fixing up a crib—all those things were there when you were born. If you have had babies (or grandchildren) of your own, you remember them all.

Then, when the baby is finally born and placed in your arms, you begin to ask questions. What will these eyes see in a lifetime? What threats and joys will come to her? Can I keep him safe? Can I afford to educate her adequately?

Do you think it was fundamentally different when Jesus was born in Bethlehem? Joseph and Mary had nervously waited. Joseph, a woodworker, had surely made a cradle and surprised Mary with it. Knowing in advance who their baby was, they had already been given his name by an angel of the Lord. Without doubt, however, they wondered about educating him, keeping him safe, and meeting the needs of the one who had come to meet everyone else's needs.

What did they see in the face of that tiny baby in Bethlehem? Imagine the scene. It was probably in a hillside cave. It would have been a relatively clean place, for animals were valued highly in that society. Away from home—without the cradle Joseph had built with such tender pride, without Mary's mother to help her with the delivery—Jesus was born.

Mary went into labor, and Joseph's calloused hands received the baby. He tied off the baby's cord, helped Mary bathe him in water warmed over a tiny fire at the mouth of the cave, and watched her wrap him in strips of linen cloth to keep him warm—the same sort of linen strips in which bodies were typically wrapped for burial in those days. Mary embraced the Resurrection and the Life in her arms.

Thus began the earthly experiences of Jesus. But what experiences they would be! Mary and Joseph could not have known, in their wildest dreams, what lay ahead for this baby.

He grew and developed normally during his early life. Luke, the physician-friend of Paul, commented twice on the growth of Jesus and gave the impression of a thoroughly normal life (cf. Luke 2:40, 52).

Unlike Greek myths and their stories of gods who walked the earth like men only to cast aside their disguise at some critical moment, Jesus really was a man. Though divine and confessed as Son of God, the title he used of himself more than any other was Son of Man. He looked like a man, talked like a man, and lived like a man. In the critical moment of his vulnera-

4

bility to death, he did not tear away his "disguise" but showed himself truly a man to the end.

He was beset by all the limitations of human beings. He was variously tired (John 4:6), hungry (Matt. 21:18), and thirsty (John 19:28). He knew, as all of us have learned, that life in a physical body is sometimes pleasant and sometimes difficult. More than that, his emotions ranged over the full spectrum of humanity. He could be joyful (John 15:11) or sorrowful (Matt. 26:37), astonished (Luke 7:9) or angry (Mark 3:5). He could love (Mark 10:21), and he could cry (John 11:35).

> His humanity does not come into view simply in times of undue difficulty. It is always there. His whole manner of life was genuinely human. As a boy He lived in subjection to Mary and Joseph (Lk. 2:51). As a man He was subject to the State and paid taxes (Mt. 17:24ff). People called Him "a glutton and a drunkard" (Mt. 11:19), and the very making of the accusation, wide of the mark though it was, shows that Jesus must have been living a full and enjoyable human life. (Leon Morris, The Lord from Heaven, 2nd ed. [Downers Grove, IL: InterVarsity Press, 1974], p. 44.)

By virtue of his real *life* as a human being, he showed us that men and women of Planet Earth are not prevented from experiencing God, honoring God, and obeying God by virtue of our humanity. He set us an example that we should follow in his steps of devotion to the Father.

Yet, with all that can be said to affirm the real humanity of Jesus Christ, the fact remains that he was

God in the flesh. He was God moving among us. He was *God* showing how much he cared about us and the lengths to which he was willing to go to redeem us.

Christians are always helping people. We present gifts to needy children. We supply food to hungry families. We arrange warm beds for homeless persons. But there are limits to what you and I are willing to do . . . or can do. I recall a Sunday night when I slept in a room with fourteen homeless men; but come Monday morning, we went our separate ways. I tried to relieve some of the burden of their homelessness, but I did not enter the full experience of it.

God has come among us! That is what Bethlehem, the manger, and the baby mean.

God entered the complete experience of our weakness, alienation, and judgment. Although he became a real man among men, he never stopped being God. He laid aside his divine rights and prerogatives, but he did not deny his nature as God. I cannot explain it to you, for I do not understand it myself. But I believe it. I stake all my hope on it—for this life and the one to come.

His words and deeds were those appropriate to God among us. Ask yourself this: If God came to live among men, what would he be like? My answer would probably be: "If God lived among us, he would never

6

sin, his words would have a unique and powerful effect on all who heard them, and his behavior would have unmistakable signs of divine presence and power." That is precisely how Jesus lived among us.

Jesus lived in such nearness to his Father and with such integrity of conscience that he could challenge his enemies with words I would never dare use: "Can any of you prove me guilty of sin?" (John 8:46). They couldn't. Neither could Judas or Pilate. Nothing his enemies ever said about him called his sinlessness of character into question.

His teaching is the absolute zenith of truth. If you have heard that his teaching was not all original and that most of it can be paralleled from rabbinic literature, such a claim is almost true yet totally false. Search the volumes of rabbinic literature, and you can glean statements similar to many of Jesus' sayings. But no rabbi, oracle, or philosopher of any age approaches him in the scope and depth of his teaching in its totality. Finding occasional colored threads of all the necessary colors is not the same as discovering a finished tapestry. All the notes are on my piano that were on Horowitz' piano, but something is noticeably different in our respective abilities to integrate and harmonize them!

Then there were Jesus' miracles. Though we are amazed by them and call them "startling" and "out of the ordinary," all the evidence seems to say that they were quite natural and unremarkable to him. If your preschool child is amazed at how bright and strong you are, it is because of a limited frame of reference. Your intelligence and strength may be quite ordinary among other adults. In the same way, we marvel at "mighty works" that, for Jesus, were Lilliputian and almost casual acts. When God dwells in flesh, we would expect mighty works to occur. That such works surrounded Jesus is no small part of the evidence that God was dwelling in flesh in his person.

God has come among us! That is what Bethlehem, the manger, and the baby mean. That is why Christians love to tell the story, sing the carols, and share the joy of the Christmas season, both with one another and with the whole world. So we still say of Jesus what Isaiah prophesied and what the angel said to Joseph, "They will call him Immanuel—which means, 'God with us'" (Matt. 1:23b).

Clifford Stewart, of Louisville, Kentucky, tells of sending his parents a microwave oven one Christmas. As he tells it:

> They were excited that now they, too, could be a part of the instant generation. When Dad unpacked the microwave and plugged it in, literally within seconds, the microwave transformed two smiles into frowns! Even after reading the directions, they couldn't make it work. Two days later, my mother was playing bridge with a friend and confessed her inability to get that microwave oven even to boil water. "To get this thing to work," she exclaimed, "I really don't need better directions; I just needed my son to come along with the gift!"

And that, my friend, is the ultimate meaning of the child in a manger at Bethlehem. When God gave the gift of salvation to us, he didn't send a book of complicated instructions for us to figure out. He sent his son.

This book is a devotional look at the characters—both at the center and on the periphery—surrounding his incarnation. May those who read its pages come to a deeper appreciation of the great mystery of God among us.

THE MEANING OF CHRISTMAS

1

THE CHRISTMAS MESSAGE

What has come to be called the "Christmas message" probably isn't. Let me explain.

The story of the birth of Jesus, as recounted in the Gospel of Luke, includes the following message from angels to shepherds at work in the open field: "Glory to God in the highest, and on earth peace, good will toward men." This rendering of the angelic announcement, from the familiar translation of the King James Version, has become known as the Christmas message.

As understood by most people and represented in art and literature, the birth of Jesus at Bethlehem was designed to bring about the cessation of hostilities, an end to war, and peace within and among nations. While the promise of national and international peace has become the general Western theme in Christmas greetings, there is good reason to think that this political and sociological theme has been read into the event.

When Jesus was born in Bethlehem, the world was at peace. The far-flung Roman legions enforced the famous *Pax Romana* that had been declared in 29 B.C. with the closing of the temple of the Roman god of war. This peace lasted until the empire began to crumble from internal decay and external conflict nearly four centuries later.

It is difficult to think that the primary purpose of the coming of Jesus could be conceived in terms of peace on the political scene. For one thing, during his adult ministry Jesus predicted that "wars and rumors of war" would continue to haunt humanity. For another, the worst wars that have ever been fought have taken place after his coming.

Properly translated from the original text, the angelic statement to the shepherds was this: "Glory to God in the highest, and on earth peace to those on whom God's favor rests." Practically all translations other than the King James Version, whether Catholic or Protestant, follow this reading.

The difference between the two readings is the difference between an unrealized promise of social peace to all persons on the one hand, and the more practical prospect of personal peace to those who receive divine favor on the other. It is the difference between public policy and personal commitment, between sociological comment and evangelistic prospect.

Although the *Pax Romana* assured political stability and freedom from war at the beginning of the Christian era, other wars raged in the human spirit. Epictetus, a Roman philosopher of the late first and early second century, observed, "While the emperor may give peace from war on land and sea, he is unable to give peace from passion, grief, and envy. He cannot give peace of heart, for which man yearns more than even for outward peace."

It was this inner peace of the human soul that the birth of Jesus made possible. Even in times of war and turmoil, believers in him have testified to inner peace attained through spiritual resources.

When a soul is at peace with her or his God, genuine peace can arise at other, larger levels. One at peace with God can be at peace with her own feelings, circumstances, and fellows. Peace can enter homes and offices. Peace could even come to an entire world.

When a soul is at peace with her or his God, genuine peace can arise at other, larger levels.

The Christmas message is one of personal peace to the individual who senses the genuine favor of God. This personal message of spiritual peace should not be politicized into the public arena. What is at stake is not only the issue of church and state in western culture but the integrity of the initial message.

The "peace on earth" that is equated with a no-more-war condition is sought by the state and prayed for by the church. The "peace on earth" that is understood as deliverance from a person's inner turmoil from a lack of spiritual meaning to his existence is possible in times of war or peace because of the birth of a baby in Bethlehem.

To believers, Jesus is not only Lord of Lords but the true Prince of Peace.

2

WHAT CHRISTMAS MEANS TO BELIEVERS

Although we cannot fix the precise date of the birth of Jesus on December 25, the indisputable fact of his historicity is beyond quibble. The late Jewish scholar, Joseph Klausner, wrote, "If we had ancient sources like those in the Gospels for the history of Alexander the Great or Julius Caesar for example, we should not cast any doubt upon them whatsoever." Only the occasional dogmatist has ever tried to assign mere mythical status to the founder of the Christian religion.

Although the nativity scenes arranged at this time of year sometimes confuse fact with folklore by putting wise men or even Santa Claus beside the manger, the child actually born into such humble circumstances has touched the world as no one else ever has. The late Will Durant, not a believer in Jesus and an agnostic on the whole God question, nevertheless wrote,

> That a few simple men should in one generation have invented so powerful and appealing a personality, so lofty an ethic and so inspiring a vision of human

brotherhood, would be a miracle far more incredible than any recorded in the Gospels. After two centuries of Higher Criticism the outlines of the life, character, and teaching of Christ, remain reasonably clear, and constitute the most fascinating feature in the history of Western man.

To those of us who do believe in the deity of Jesus, the fact that the world still celebrates his birth nearly two thousand years after the event is a strong proof of his identity as the Son of God.

Some in his own day and even now regard Jesus merely as "the carpenter's son." But carpenters don't know how to turn water into wine, or make the lame walk and the blind see. They can make yokes or plows. But what of healing broken lives and forgiving sins? These are not the gifts of a carpenter's son.

Others see him only as "the son of Mary." Yes, she was his mother, a woman of virtue and devotion to God. But Mary had other sons who were not like this one. He had no flaws in his character. His teachings never had to be corrected, amended, or apologized for. Yes, he was a son to Mary. But he was more.

No poet, no dreamer, no philosopher ever loved people as he loved them. He exploited no one and blessed all. His Sermon on the Mount is regarded as the zenith of spiritual instruction and a masterpiece of literature by friend and foe alike.

No foolish words came from his mouth. Not a single foolish deed marred his career. When he was unjustly put on trial for his life, perjured witnesses could not get their stories straight. Sullen and disinterested

Pilate, in a rare moment of integrity, told the mob, "There is no fault in him."

There is no one like him in the annals of history. As a teacher, as a doer of good deeds, as a moral philosopher—he has no equal. Even among those who have tried hardest to imitate him, all would admit how faulty their imitations have been. In his very person, he stands as the greatest miracle of the ages.

It defies the facts to think of him as a mere mortal. He is without doubt the Son of God.

Who, then, was Jesus? Whose son is he? It defies the facts to think of him as a mere mortal. He is without doubt the Son of God. Apart from his deity, he could not have made the impact on history that he did.

No mind but an infinite one could have known what he knew. No heart but an infinite one could have loved as he loved. No benefactor but an infinite one could have given the free gift of eternal life he gives.

Let his coming into the world be celebrated on December 25. But let it be celebrated also on every other day of the year.

ANTICIPATION

3
WHEN THE TIME CAME

I've wondered about it. Did an alarm sound? Did a specially commissioned angel step forward and announce that it was time to go? Did the voice of God thunder across heaven and call everyone to a bon voyage party for the one who would soon be known on Earth as Jesus?

I know the pain it causes us mortals to see someone off. Remember the day your daughter got married? Did you have to send your husband or fiance off to war? Have you sent a son away to college? The time finally came, but it wasn't easy, was it? The day had long been marked on your calendar in red ink. A special reminder of the time of departure was written and posted in a conspicuous place. Maybe a tear stained the calendar as you tried to circle the date. Partings are hard, even if they have been planned for a long time.

Father, Son, and Holy Spirit had all agreed that the journey would have to be made. No one else could do what needed to be done. The Son had volunteered, and the time had been set from eternity past. Now the day had arrived. Family partings are difficult even in the divine family.

Where would he go? To an intellectual capital such as Athens? To the power seat of Rome? Perhaps to the critical Old Testament city of Jerusalem. What a shock it must have been for Gabriel or Michael to discover that Bethlehem, a little town in Judea, had been chosen for the first stop.

> *The Son had volunteered, and the time had been set from eternity past.*

How would he make the trip? An angelic escort was surely in order. His passage would probably be trailed by lightning, fire, and smoke. Perhaps there would be a flaming chariot. Instead, God chose to send the Son into the world of human experience via the womb of a teenage Jewish peasant girl from Nazareth named Mary, only recently betrothed to a carpenter in the same town.

What sort of life would he experience? Would he live in a palace? How many servants would be required? Might his opulent splendor make people forget Solomon's legendary glory? No, he would grow up in a nondescript village named Nazareth, get a bit of education from the teacher at the town's synagogue, play with children on the outskirts of town, and learn to make yokes and plows and stools in Joseph's wood-working shop.

How would humankind react to his presence? Certainly, the world would acclaim his coming. Likely everyone would declare allegiance to him, and be perfectly loyal to him. Against these reasonable expectations, rejection and death on a Roman cross lay ahead.

So what would be the outcome of this public-relations fiasco? Could he at least get a decent burial plot and a substantial marker? Would any movement he might initiate survive it? Might vengeance from the Father and Holy Spirit against the enemies of the Son follow? The truth is that his death brought salvation and the full rights of sonship to all who will receive him through faith in and obedience to the gospel.

There was probably neither gong nor party. Perhaps there were just whispered words: "It's time. I'll miss you and will be anxious for you to get back home. While you are away, remember that I love you—and them."

In that subdued moment, all of heaven learned that the time had fully come. The events that would enact the greatest rescue effort of the ages were now in motion.

4

AN AIR OF EXPECTATION

The birth of Jesus was the best-prepared-for event in the history of the world. You'd have never suspected that, though, by watching the events unfold. Everything looked so haphazard, so unarranged, so chancy. But it was the working out of a divine plan.

Long before Mary gave birth to her first child, God had been preparing for the event in countless ways. Most of those workings were unannounced and unobserved, but many stand in bold relief in the biblical record.

No sooner had Adam and Eve sinned than heaven began dropping hints of the coming redeemer. In his rebuke of the tempter in Eden, Yahweh said, "And I will put enmity between you and the woman, and between your offspring and hers; he will crush your head, and you will strike his heel" (Gen. 3:15). We call this statement the *protoevangelium,* for it strikes the note of promise and hope at the very outset of redemptive history.

Later God announced that he would send the promised redeemer through Abraham, Isaac, and Jacob and that he would be a Jew. More specifically still, he revealed that the "scepter will not depart from Judah, nor the ruler's staff from between his feet, until he comes to whom it belongs and the obedience of the nations is his" (Gen. 49:10).

Isaiah spoke for the Lord to say that a "virgin will be with child and will give birth to a son" (Isa. 7:14). That son would be Immanuel, "God with us" in the sense of God being manifest in flesh and living as a member of the human race. God revealed to the prophet Micah that the Messiah's birthplace would be David's city of Bethlehem (Mic. 5:2).

But it was not only the Jewish world that had been affected by the divine workings. The larger Roman world was also occupied with a strong sense of expectancy about the coming of a Great King at the very time when Jesus appeared.

The historian Suetonius wrote shortly after Jesus' day and said, "There had spread over all the Orient an old and established belief, that it was fated at that time for men coming from Judea to rule the world" (*Life of Vespasian.* 4. 5). Tacitus also knew the tradition that "there was a firm persuasion . . . that at this very time the East was to grow powerful, and rulers coming from Judea were to acquire universal empire" (*Histories.* 5. 13).

Josephus, the Jew who saved his own neck by betraying his nation, wrote histories of the Jews for his Roman benefactors. He did not fail to point out that the Jewish people believed that "about that time one from their country should become governor of the habitable earth" (*Wars of the Jews*. 6. 5. 4).

At practically the same time that Jesus was born at Bethlehem, the Roman Emperor, Augustus, was being hailed as the Savior of the World. And Palestine's Roman puppet, Herod the Great, had taken the title "King of the Jews" to himself.

The world was in eager anticipation. Men and women from all backgrounds and races were longing for God or God's anointed Savior to appear. They believed that God was going to move in history, identify a redeemer, and inaugurate a Golden Age.

Beyond mere anticipation, however, the world was in a unique and unprecedented state of readiness for the appearance of Jesus. The old Greco-Roman polytheism had broken down. Both pagan and Jewish societies felt a sense of spiritual vacuum and wanted it filled. Honor was dying. Moral standards were incredibly low, and the personal behavior of both emperor and peasant was abominable.

The Roman Empire was enforcing peace throughout the Mediterranean World and, for the sake of its legions, had linked the empire's far-flung parts by clearing the seas of pirates and building excellent roads. And, while every province preserved its own language or dialect, Greek was the common tongue of the empire. Practically everyone was bilingual and could communicate with everyone else.

No wonder Paul could say that God acted to send the Son at just the proper juncture of history. "But when the time had fully come, God sent his Son, born of a woman, born under law, to redeem those under law, that we might receive the full rights of sons" (Gal. 4:4-5).

Out of the depths of eternity came the Son of God. At the perfect time—not a moment too early and not a moment too late—he appeared as the embodiment of grace and truth. The plan that had been in the mind of God from eternity became real in the arena of human history.

> Beyond all question, the mystery of godliness is great:
> He appeared in a body,
>   was vindicated by the Spirit,
>   was preached among the nations,
>   was believed on in the world,
>   was taken up in glory. (1 Tim. 3:16)

The plan that had been in the mind of God from eternity became real in the arena of human history.

Men and women of every generation in history have been affected by Jesus Christ. Those who lived long before his birth at Bethlehem were moved by the prophetic anticipations of his coming. They "searched intently and with the greatest care" to try to understand what the predictions meant and to recognize the one who would fulfill them when he appeared (1 Pet. 1:10-12).

During his lifetime, people, families, whole cities, and even entire races of people were touched by his powerful life. In the centuries following, he continues to draw people to himself.

It cannot be explained by money, formal education, military force, or political clout. It can only be accounted for by the fact of his deity. "The Word became flesh and made his dwelling among us. We have seen his glory, the glory of the One and Only, who came from the Father, full of grace and truth" (John 1:14).

MARY

5

A FRIGHTENED LITTLE GIRL

She had been with some of her teenage girlfriends all day. There had been lots of giggling, with no small amount of it prompted by her. There had also been some envy, prompted by the same thing that had made them giggle. At age fourteen, Mary was engaged to be married. Her playmates wanted to know about Joseph, about the wedding feast that was still several months away, and about Mary's feelings.

There was nothing unusual about the situation. Girls in Nazareth were considered eligible for marriage at thirteen. To reach the age of fifteen or sixteen without arrangements for a suitable husband was humiliating. Mary would be spared the fate of being thought undesirable or of being teased for having no husband.

She both loved and feared the God of Israel. Believing that her people were the covenant people of Yahweh who would someday see the Lord's Messiah in their midst, she felt an abiding sense of love for Israel's Bridegroom in her life. What a wonderful thought! Israel was to Yahweh what she was to Joseph!

Knowing that Yahweh could punish or exclude from Israel's covenant promises any Israelite who defied his holy commandments, she revered the Torah and had pledged herself early in life to live in obedience to its requirements.

For Mary, as with every pious girl in Israel, it had been particularly important for her to preserve her virginity and reputation. She felt fully rewarded for doing so by being selected as the wife of so good and decent a man as Joseph, a respected carpenter in Nazareth. She was only beginning to get acquainted with him, for first-century marriages did not come at the end of a dating ritual. Families arranged these unions, and women in particular had no real say in the matter. Mary trusted her father's love. She knew that he would choose her husband carefully and with much prayer. From all she had come to learn about Joseph, there was no doubt that the carpenter was God's gift to her, the answer to her own as well as her parents' prayers.

But now, resting alone in her family's one-room house, Mary suddenly felt uneasy. It was the sort of feeling one sometimes gets when she feels that someone else has come into the room. Was someone else here? Were somebody's eyes fixed on her? She turned to look.

She *wasn't* alone! A man was in the house. She had never seen him before. He didn't look threatening or sinister, but he was in her house. And she was alone. Her heart raced and she flinched. Clutching her robe to her breast, she drew away and turned her eyes.

"Don't be afraid, Mary," said the man, "you have found favor with God" (Luke 1:30).

"He knows my name," she thought to herself. "And what a strange greeting. Men sometimes receive calls from God, but I am a woman, really only a girl getting ready to learn about being a woman. Oh, if only Joseph were here to protect me!"

Yet she was conscious of the strange fact that she no longer really felt uncomfortable with this man. Daring to raise her eyes again and look at him more closely, she didn't know how to describe the look on his face. And she was captivated by his eyes. With their dark and gentle gaze, those eyes gave her the impression that they could see into eternity.

Could this possibly be an angel rather than a mere mortal? She believed in angels. But why would an angel be speaking to her? As Mary wrestled with her whirring thoughts, the strange visitor, seeming less threatening the longer she looked at him, spoke again.

"You will be with child and give birth to a son, and you are to give him the name Jesus," he said. "He will be great and will be called the Son of the Most High. The Lord God will give him the throne of his father David, and he will reign over the house of Jacob forever; his kingdom will never end" (Luke 1:31-33).

Mary had dreamed about having a baby. She and her friends had talked about what the experience might be like less than an hour ago! But it just couldn't be. Joseph had never touched her—and no other man ever would!

"How will this be?" Mary gasped. "I am a virgin!"(Luke 1:34).

Without hesitation and with the most confident tone she had ever heard, her angel-guest replied, "The

Holy Spirit will come upon you, and the power of the
Most High will overshadow you. So the holy one to be
born will be called the Son of God" (Luke 1:35).

Mary must have wondered if it were all a dream, a
concern that only occurs to people who are awake and
alert. Maybe she pinched herself, shook her head, or
rubbed her eyes. By this time, she may have felt secure
enough to reach out and touch him.

---

*If the child was not to be
fathered by Joseph, what
would he think of her
pregnancy?*

It really *was* happening! An angel from God was
telling her that she had been chosen to be the mother
of the Messiah. She remembered hearing one of the
girls from Nazareth say that her dream was to have a
son who would be Israel's redeemer. Mary had been
frightened at the thought. She had wondered at the
time whether the girl had blasphemed. She had never
dared to utter such a thought, which nevertheless ran
through the mind of every daughter of Israel.

Mary's only thought of late had been of bearing
Joseph's children. Joseph! What did the angel's words
mean in relation to him? If the child was not to be fathered by Joseph, what would he think of her pregnancy? How would he react? She feared she knew the
answer to her own questions. She feared she knew

how Joseph, her own family, and the people of Nazareth would interpret a swollen belly on a fourteen-year-old, unmarried girl.

Some would say horrible things about Joseph, the best man Mary had ever met and who was honorable in everything. She could not bear the thought of ruining the reputation of the man to whom she was pledged. And would Joseph himself believe Mary's explanation? Could he? Could anyone who had not seen this angel and heard his voice accept her account of what was to happen?

How could this be? It was impossible for a virgin to become pregnant and bear a child! If this were truly about to happen, surely a sign would be given.

Then, as if he had been reading her every thought, the angel told Mary, "Even Elizabeth your relative is going to have a child in her old age, and she who was said to be barren is in her sixth month" (Luke 1:36). She had not heard about her cousin Elizabeth being pregnant. It would be an easy thing to find out. Was that to be Mary's sign? Would Elizabeth understand what was happening to Mary? Could she explain it to Mary? Would she and her priest-husband help her explain it to Joseph? Then the angel finished by saying, "For nothing is impossible with God" (Luke 1:37).

Mary wanted to ask, "*What* is not impossible for God? For Elizabeth to be pregnant at her age? For me, a virgin, to have a baby? For Joseph to believe me?"

You'll have to admit that this choice makes no sense. If someone was to give birth to and be responsible for the Son of God, surely it should be someone older, perhaps Elizabeth, and someone with experience in taking care of babies. The thought of a teenage girl giving birth to God-come-into-flesh and perhaps taking care of him without a husband is an absurdity. But many of God's doings in history have looked absurd to us: Mt. Moriah, the Red Sea, Jericho, Mt. Carmel—the list goes on and on.

Can Mary agree to this? Can a frightened little girl have enough faith to take all the risks involved? What will she do? Or has she been chosen precisely because she is still a child? Young people have such a capacity for faith. It is the later cynicism that becomes such a stumbling block for so many of us.

"I am the Lord's servant," Mary told the angel. "May it be to me as you have said" (Luke 1:38).

The angel smiled, said nothing, and left Mary alone with her thoughts. And what thoughts they were! "If there is anyone with whom I can share this," she thought, "it is my cousin Elizabeth. I must go to see her."

So she began her trip to the little town in the hill country of Judea where Elizabeth lived. As she traveled, she thought. She may have cried. She sifted every detail of the angel's announcement.

She could not know what lay ahead. All she knew with absolute certainty was what she had told the angel. She was the Lord's. She was ready to serve him in whatever way God wished to be served. She did not understand God and his ways, but she believed in Yahweh and would sacrifice herself to be his servant. She did not know then that her heart would be pierced for her son. She had no idea that she would someday be left standing beside his dead body to feel all over again in her fifties the fear and confusion of this day in her teens.

The same can be said of any one of us. When we surrender to let God have his way in our lives, we cannot know what lies ahead. We can only wait in faith for him to work all things together to his own ends and purposes.

Can a frightened little girl have enough faith to take all the risks involved?

When Mary arrived at the home of Zechariah and Elizabeth, she received the sign that confirmed her faith in the angel's announcement to her.

> When Elizabeth heard Mary's greeting, the baby leaped in her womb, and Elizabeth was filled with the Holy Spirit. In a loud voice she exclaimed: "Blessed are you among women, and blessed is the child you will bear! But why am I so favored, that the mother of my Lord should come to me? As soon as the sound of your greeting reached my ears, the baby in my womb leaped for joy. Blessed is she who has believed that what the Lord has said to her will be accomplished!" (Luke 1:41-45)

By the spirit of prophecy that came to Elizabeth, the message of the angel was confirmed. Mary had been specially chosen of God and was "blessed among women"; Mary would have a child, and that child would be divine. As double confirmation to Mary, she found Elizabeth well along in her own pregnancy, just as the angel had told her.

At some point during their time together, Elizabeth surely told Mary the details of the miraculous events connected with her pregnancy. Elizabeth's husband, Zechariah, while serving at the altar of incense as priest, had been confronted by the angel Gabriel. Gabriel told him that his prayer for a child had been heard, that his aged Elizabeth would bear his son, and that the boy's name was to be John (Luke 1:8-13).

Gabriel had also indicated something of the career John would have within Israel. He would "go on before the Lord, in the spirit and power of Elijah" for the purpose of creating a "people prepared for the Lord" (Luke 1:14-17). There can be little doubt that Zechariah and Elizabeth saw the messianic import of that announcement. John's presence in the spirit of Elijah would bring to mind the language of Malachi 4:5 and was a promise of Messiah's appearance.

The good priest Zechariah, however, had a hard time believing the angel and asked for a sign (Luke 1:18). Because of Zechariah's disbelief, Gabriel announced that he would be unable to speak until the child was born (Luke 1:19-22). Elizabeth immediately became pregnant and remained in seclusion most of the time (Luke 1:23-25). Zechariah's speech did not return until the circumcision and naming of his son (Luke 1:59-64).

The shared prospect of giving birth to sons linked the two women in spirit. The cousins would have sons who, by virtue of an anointing from God rather than mere ties of family, would bring the hopes of Israel to fulfillment. Mary stayed with Elizabeth for about three months, apparently returning to Nazareth just before the birth of John (Luke 1:56). The time they shared must have been without precedent in the history of the human race. What excitement there would have been in their conversations! What anticipations they had! What apprehension must have filled the air!

The Scriptures tell us that when Mary first saw Elizabeth, she expressed her joy in a prophetic song through the inspiration of the Holy Spirit.

> My soul glorifies the Lord
>   and my spirit rejoices in God my Savior,
> for he has been mindful
>   of the humble state of his servant.
> From now on all generations will call me blessed,
>   for the Mighty One has done great
>   things for me—
>   holy is his name.
> His mercy extends to those who fear him,
>   from generation to generation.
> He has performed mighty deeds with his arm;
>   he has scattered those who are proud in
>   their inmost thoughts.
> He has brought down rulers from their thrones
>   but has lifted up the humble.
> He has filled the hungry with good things
>   but has sent the rich away empty.
> He has helped his servant Israel,
>   remembering to be merciful
> to Abraham and his descendants forever,
>   even as he said to our fathers.
>   (Luke 1:46b-55)

The frightened teenager of Bethlehem became the mother of the Lord Jesus Christ. Her love must have been tender, gentle, and formative. No one less than the purest and best of womankind would have been chosen for this role.

While Roman Catholic doctrines about Mary have tended to push many of us away from this wonderful saint, we must not resist Scripture or denigrate her by failing to give honor where honor is due. Without embracing fanciful legends that grew up in later centuries around the name of Mary, we can still acknowledge the virgin of Nazareth whose self-sacrifice to God's purpose teaches all of us to be servants to the Lord.

6
MARY'S FIRST CHILD

As with every other girl she had known while growing up in Nazareth, Mary dreamed of getting married and having a baby. But the reality of this night had never been part of those fantasies.

There had been no baby showers for Mary or celebrations of the impending birth with neighbors. But there had been much whispering, some furtive glances in her direction, and even some snickering by girlfriends from her recent past. The pregnancy had not been difficult physically, but it had been an emotionally draining nine months.

The birth itself had not been in Nazareth. Her mother was not with her. There hadn't even been a midwife. She and Joseph had been alone in a place meant for animals rather than people.

Joseph had been wonderful to her. He made her a clean place and prepared as comfortable a bed as he could. He had been nervous. You could tell that he was hoping the baby would not come tonight. When the pains started, however, he was calm. And his huge, strong, carpenter's hands had been as gentle as possible as he helped Mary give birth to the son he had not fathered.

The two of them wrapped strips of cloth they had brought from Nazareth around the baby's limbs and torso to keep him warm in the night. As countless parents have done before and since, they counted fingers and toes. They gazed into each other's eyes and spoke of their love for each other and the child. They prayed and thanked Yahweh for choosing them to be the parents of the tiny boy received in a stable and laid in a manger.

The child who had just come from her body had come to her womb from the throne room of heaven.

Now the infant was sleeping beside Mary. Add to the feelings every mother has about the miracle of her baby's birth the special knowledge she had of an angel's visit, a miraculous conception, and Joseph's dream, and Mary must have been in awe. Exhausted and still in pain from delivering the baby, she was nonetheless aware that the child who had just come from her body had come to her womb from the throne room of heaven. When she did finally fall into peaceful sleep, what did she dream?

Could she have imagined the tension that would develop in her own family as this child's younger brothers would one day taunt him for his dreams?

Surely, on that special night, she could not have dreamed of the rejection Jesus would suffer in Nazareth and Jerusalem from the most powerful men of Israel.

And it cannot have come to her mind that she would, about thirty-five years from this night, stand helplessly by and watch him die horribly on a Roman cross.

Tonight she could only be happy and feel close to God. She experienced a sense of peace within the divine scheme of things that few people in the history of the world would ever know.

Mary had just given birth to the Son of God, the Messiah, Immanuel. Every time she awoke that night, she would look at him and whisper his name, as if saying it so many times would make it and the child fit each other. "Jesus. Jesus. Jesus."

She knew that the drama of the life of her first child had only just begun.

7

SOME PARADOXES OF MOTHERHOOD

What would it have been like to be the mother of the Son of God? That she was a special woman with deep reserves of character and faith surely goes without saying. Heaven could not have chosen just anyone to be the mother of God's beloved son.

Even so, Mary's days with her son were probably as mixed and uneven as mothers' days are today. A host of things happened in Mary's life that are fairly typical of a mother's experience at any time and with any child.

On some days, Mary must have been *puzzled*.

Although an angel had announced it, Mary was bewildered that she could be pregnant though still a virgin. Her time with Zechariah and Elizabeth added more astounding events to her swirling mind. That shepherds neither she nor her husband knew or had ever seen before would show up on the night her son Jesus was born at Bethlehem was no small thing either. Upon their arrival, they added to the larger mystery by telling about angels they had seen that night and by whose direction they were present at the stable-birthing room.

When she and Joseph carried Jesus into the temple compound for the first time, Simeon recognized the baby as the long-awaited Messiah of Israel. Yet he proceeded to tell Mary that he would be spoken against and said to her, "And a sword will pierce your own soul too" (Luke 2:35b).

Then Gentile strangers appeared unexpectedly from the East and brought expensive gifts—gold, frankincense, and myrrh—to her son.

Because of King Herod's jealous rage, several baby boys at Bethlehem were murdered by soldiers. She, Joseph, and Jesus fled to Egypt because of a warning from God. Was this horrible slaughter of innocent infants the heartache Simeon had predicted? Would there be other things as bad, or possibly worse, for her to face because of his presence in her world? It was as if those babies had died in Jesus' place or had been sacrificed on account of his birth. (What irony from our perspective!)

No wonder the Bible says that Mary "treasured up" events like these from her son's life and "pondered them in her heart" (Luke 2:19).

On most days, however, Mary's heart surely chose to dwell on the *promise* of her little boy.

Oh, she must have dreamed the sorts of things mothers always imagine about their babies. She tried to visualize him as a grown man—robust, dignified, acclaimed, sought after. He would certainly be the leading citizen of Israel. No, he would be the most celebrated personality in the world!

She probably worried a bit about how she would handle the adulation and fuss people might make over her because her son would be sitting on the throne of David. Modest and godly woman that she was, she prayed that he would not have his head turned by the wealth and prestige that would come to him. Little did she know!

About the time Jesus hit early adolescence, Mary's pride in her firstborn son was often tinged with *perplexity*. And that would be the case often as he grew up and lived a life very different from the one she would have dreamed or chosen for him.

Why, when he was twelve, he stayed behind the group that his family was traveling with after Passover in Jerusalem. When she found him and asked "Son, why have you treated us like this?" his answer stung her a bit. "Why were you searching for me? Didn't you know I had to be in my Father's house?" (Luke 2:48-49). Did he really think it unreasonable for her and Joseph to go looking for their boy who was playing hooky?

Mary endured episodes of *pain* for her son's sake.

Her beloved Joseph was about to break their betrothal and divorce her—until an angel of the Lord explained her pregnancy to him. When the time came for her baby to be born, she was seventy miles away from her home, her family, and the midwife she had planned to have help her with the delivery. And, of all places, she was in an animal shelter and had to use a feeding trough filled with hay for a crib.

Neither did she escape the grief of being taunted over the circumstances of Jesus' birth. The people of

Nazareth who knew Joseph and Mary did not know their account of the premarital pregnancy. Furthermore, they could not have believed it had they known it. True to form, Mary was the object of more public talk than Joseph. Then, when Jesus began his public work, she heard the reports of people calling him an illegitimate child. She wept for Jesus, and she wept for herself.

Her home would not always be peaceful over the next twenty or so years, and you know the kind of pain family turmoil gives a mother's heart. Jesus' younger brothers would not believe what Mary said about him or the claims their elder brother eventually made for himself. It would create some nasty scenes that would break any mother's heart.

But the ultimate pain would be Golgotha, that infamous "Place of the Skull." How thankful I am that she could not foresee that awful day while she cradled the tiny babe in her arms—nursing him at her breasts, tracing her soft fingers around the delicate curves of his ear, and whispering "I love you." Only on that painful day would she understand what had been involved in Simeon's prediction about her soul being pierced with a sword.

Mothers, does any of this sound familiar? You have marvelled both at the wonder of birth and at the impact that single event can have on every other person, event, and thing in your life.

You have dreamed the dreams that can arise only within the heart of a baby's mother—seeing her in your mind's eye all grown up, envisioning what he will be like and what he will do. You fear to share some of those dreams with anyone lest you be laughed at, but you still cherish them and love to dream them.

Like Mary, you have also had occasion to be perplexed. You've worried about grades and friendships and influences. You've agonized over their attempts to spread their wings and establish their own identity. And you have fought the fear of rejection from your son or daughter at this critical right of passage.

How thankful I am that she could not foresee that awful day while she cradled the tiny babe in her arms.

And, yes, you may have felt the pain that sons such as myself have caused you. You have watched every labored, fevered breath in the nights when we were sick. You have ached for us when we suffered a major disappointment with life. You have cried yourselves to sleep when we have been rebels and prodigals, doing foolish things, getting into trouble with the law, hurting ourselves with irresponsible behavior.

Like Mary, though, you have always been there. You have never stopped praying for God's will to be done in our lives. You have hurt more for us than we could realize or understand. You have taken immeasurable pride in our accomplishments.

I wish we knew more of how Jesus communicated his love to Mary. That might help some of us do a better job in making our love for you more conspicuous.

I do know this much, however. After her son's resurrection and ascension, she was with the apostles in the upper room. By that time she understood that her own suffering for her son, through all the bewildering experiences of his life and their sometimes confusing relationship, had had a purpose.

Her faithfulness to him had been tested for well over thirty-five years. But mothers are just that way. They can be patient with their children. The issue is not the speed with which things are resolved, but simply that they are resolved and that things turn out right for their sons and daughters.

Mary lived to see her original joy and amazement return full circle. If your experiences as a mother are ever confusing or dismal with your beloved children, I pray that God will grant you the same happy fulfillment.

JOSEPH

8
THE DEVOUT CARPENTER

Joseph was spending this Sabbath as he spent every other. This was the established weekly holy day for him and his people. He was never even tempted to keep his carpenter's shop open on Saturdays.

No matter how much work there was to be done, no matter how many of his customers were clamoring for yokes, plows, or tables, no matter how much he needed the income from another day's work, the Sabbath belonged to the Lord. Before three stars could be seen in the sky on Friday, the tools of his trade were put away. The pleasant smells of sawdust and wood shavings were surrendered in favor of the sights and sounds of the Nazareth synagogue.

The service began today, as always, with a recitation of the ancient Shema. This familiar call to prayer and worship reminded Joseph and the other worshippers why they had assembled: "Hear, O Israel: The Lord our God, the Lord is one. Love the Lord your God with all your heart and with all your soul and with all your strength" (Deut. 6:4-9, 11:13-21; Num. 15:37-41).

There had been a prayer, followed by a reading from the Torah and then one from the Prophets. He had learned to love the words of these sacred texts as a boy in this same synagogue. The language he had learned from daily use in his parents' home was Aramaic, spoken by his people since the time of their captivity in Babylon. But the Hebrew tongue in which Scripture was preserved was important enough that the sons of most devout families still studied it. With many boys his own age, he had learned ancient Hebrew here. Though not scholarly enough to be a synagogue reader, he loved to hear the words intoned each week from the synagogue scrolls.

He listened more intently now as the completed readings were translated into his everyday Aramaic. He hung on every word, believing that they were the words of Yahweh as communicated through human vessels. From week to week, various rabbis presented brief discourses they had prepared on the readings. The quality of the presentations was a bit uneven, but Joseph was the sort of man who would listen with the humility of one who believed he could learn something from any rabbi who spoke. He was not a rabbi, but he secretly dreamed that one or more of the sons he hoped to have might be.

Today Joseph's mind was wandering a bit. It wasn't that the layman-teacher (the rabbis were learned men of the community rather than ordained, professional teachers) was doing a poor job or that Joseph was uninterested in the study of Scripture. But as he drew near the synagogue today, he had caught a glimpse of Mary. She was always in his thoughts. Now that he had seen her at a distance, his mind was hopelessly preoccupied.

Until today, he had not seen Mary for three months. Unaware that she was planning to leave Nazareth, he had suddenly missed her. Her family told him that she had gone to visit a cousin who lived about seventy miles away in the hill country of Judea. Joseph had sensed that even they were somewhat mystified by her trip. She and her cousin, who was old enough to be her mother, had never been particularly close that anyone recalled, but it had seemed suddenly important for Mary to see her.

As he sat in his appointed place near the back of the synagogue (the oldest and most distinguished men sat in the front seats), he could see her face. Oh, not literally, for males and females were always separated from each other by a screen during the service. But his mind kept calling up images of her beautiful features.

Joseph had always respected Mary's family. Then, as he began to notice her in particular, he was impressed with a maturity that seemed beyond her years. She worked and played with the girls her own age, yet she somehow seemed set apart from them in Joseph's mind. So, when the time came for Joseph to choose a bride, he had no great difficulty. Among the few marriageable girls of Nazareth, any other was a distant second choice for him. He made his wishes known to his family, and there had been no dissent. The arrangements between the families of Joseph and Mary were made quickly and with eagerness.

The formal betrothal of the two had been a day of exquisite joy for them. Joseph felt a sense of pride in this public declaration of his financial and social right to create his own family and to assume the responsibility for it. And he was proud of Mary, knowing that many other men his age who were contemplating marriage also saw her desirability.

The synagogue service moved toward its conclusion. The whole assembly sang together. Some of the favorite psalms of the Nazareth synagogue were sung in their customary antiphonal manner. The cantor then sang a short section, and the whole group responded in unison. Some of the songs were so familiar to Joseph and the others that they could have sung them without the cantor's promptings.

Then, with the closing prayers and benedictions, the service ended, and the assembly dismissed. Some stood inside or near the door to talk, but Joseph had no time for idle conversation today. He moved outside quickly and stood where he could watch the worshippers as they left. He wanted to see Mary, to speak to her, to let her know how much he had missed her. He wanted to ask about her visit with her cousin. Did he have her name right? He recalled that Mary's father had called her Elizabeth.

Yet he knew he could not say all he wanted to say or ask too many questions. There was propriety to consider. For his own sake and for hers, any conversation would have to be brief. It would be best if several family members were nearby. Although they were engaged to be married, custom did not allow them time alone with each other. All that would have to wait until after the marriage proper.

As a man significantly older than Mary, Joseph felt it was more his responsibility than hers to be sure that their relationship was kept absolutely honorable. There would be no indiscretions. There would be no invitations to whisperers. This righteous man would act as a son of the covenant should toward his betrothed, and there would be no hint of anything improper between them.

Then he saw her. She was the same beautiful girl his mind had conjured up during the synagogue service. But somehow she was different, too. Her smile seemed a bit nervous. Her eyes had a sense of pleading about them. And she was walking directly toward him. Had something happened while she was away? Was there bad news about her cousin or her family?

"Joseph," said Mary, "we must talk. There is something you have to know. I cannot bear to keep it from you any longer, but I fear what you may do."

Something was wrong, terribly wrong. Joseph's heartbeat quickened, and he felt his face begin to flush. He was conscious that his big hands were tightening into tense fists and that his whole body was coming taut. What was so terrible in Mary's mind that she was both anxious to tell him and afraid of his response?

Could she be having second thoughts about their marriage. Was she frightened of leaving home or of becoming his wife? Perhaps it was some horrible news from her cousin's home, a death or family tragedy. Had there been some scandal that Mary feared would reflect on Joseph? But, no, her cousin lived seventy miles away; any scandal in her cousin's life would not intimidate him from so far away. In all likelihood, few in Nazareth would ever hear of it.

Yes, they needed to talk. And Joseph would be patient with the teenager's fears without seeming to condescend. If there was bad news from Judea, he would set her mind at ease. He would express sympathy and concern and reassure her that nothing happening that far away would be an obstacle to their plans here in Nazareth.

Joseph discreetly stepped back and motioned for Mary to walk a few steps with him away from the people. Yet he was careful that they not walk too far away, stand in shadows, or seem clandestine. Propriety could not be abandoned. Joseph was big on propriety. So, while respecting Mary's request to talk with him, he would not forget that others would have to see that their behavior was above reproach.

"What is so heavy on your heart?" he asked. "I have missed you and would like to talk with you about your trip. Is that what you want to talk about?"

Mary didn't look at Joseph. She stared at the ground. A sense of panic rose in her spirit, and she began to doubt that she could speak at all. She wondered if she had made a mistake in asking to talk with him. Perhaps she should have tried to talk with her own family first, then allow one of them to talk with Joseph.

Joseph interrupted her thoughts and spoke again. He almost reached out to touch her shoulder and turn her body directly toward himself, but he caught himself immediately. That would not be proper. Joseph's parents had taught him that propriety in a man's relationship with a woman is all important. He would not step over that invisible boundary, even though he felt an instinctive compassion for the agony of soul he sensed in Mary. For the first time in months, he saw her again as a little girl. She was scared and confused and about to cry.

A sense of panic rose in her spirit, and she began to doubt that she could speak at all.

"Mary, please tell me. Perhaps I can help," he said. "Surely there is nothing so terrible as you are imagining this to be."

"Joseph," she said, looking into his eyes now for the first time since she spoke to him, "I am going to have a baby. It was announced to me by an angel and confirmed to me by my cousin Elizabeth. Joseph, the baby I am carrying does not belong to a human father but was placed in my womb by the Spirit of God."

He heard himself gasp, and he saw the anxious look on Mary's face as she looked away from him in the direction of the synagogue. Joseph immediately connected what Mary had said with the synagogue. Had she been guilty of blasphemy today by daring to enter it? How could she enter that holy place of worship in her condition? And how dare she concoct such a story to explain her unfaithfulness to him! How dare she speak of a baby conceived by the Spirit of God!

Joseph's mind raced. "How could she betray me like this?" "How could I have been so wrong about her?" "Who is the father of her baby?" "What should I do?" "How can I stand the embarrassment and humiliation when this becomes a matter of public record?" "Will people think that I am responsible for her pregnancy?"

How dare she concoct such a story to explain her unfaithfulness to him!

Joseph's theory had always been that faithful sons of Israel were spared such shame. It was too much for him to take in at once. He had no response for Mary. He didn't know what to say to her. He simply turned away and walked toward home. He had never been so confused in all his life.

Over the next couple of days, Joseph did not see Mary. As a matter of fact, he purposely avoided any place where she might be. He had to be alone. He had to think. He had to make the hardest decision of his life.

During the day, he worked to the point of exhaustion in his shop. Yet hard work was not enough to drive the matter out of his mind. The few people who came by his shop were not really welcome, for he was in no mood for small talk.

The nights were harder still. In spite of a full day of hard work, he did not sleep well. What sleep there was came in short snatches—fitful and restless. So he prayed. He tried to recall what the Torah said about such cases and how they were to be handled. What was the proper thing for him to do?

As things appeared, Joseph had no choice. As a devout Israelite, he would have to end his relationship with Mary. He would have to divorce her. Yet the very thought of going through with it made him sick at his stomach. He had no real fear of Mary being stoned, though the Law of Moses provided for the death penalty in such cases. That sentence had not been executed in Israel for generations in adultery cases. And with Rome reserving the death penalty to its own courts, that would not happen.

Other things would happen to Mary, though, and thoughts of them bothered Joseph terribly. For starters, there would be shame and expulsion from the community. Disgrace would extend to her entire family. He had unpleasant visions of Mary caring for an illegitimate child. He knew that most women in those circumstances wound up supporting themselves either by selling themselves into slavery or by becoming prostitutes.

Was it possible that Mary's story was true? Could an angel have told her that she was bearing a child for God? Joseph knew the story of Sarah's son in her old age and of Hannah's child after painful years of infertility. But Abraham and Elkanah were the fathers of those children. There was no precedent in Hebrew history or Scripture for a virginal conception.

Apparently he had been wrong about Mary all along. Perhaps she was crazy. But he would not—no, could not—accept her farfetched story.

Joseph was therefore torn between the conflicting demands of law and love. There was no doubt that he still loved Mary. Yet neither was there any doubt as to what he must do. His heart wanted to believe anything that would exonerate Mary and allow him to have her as his wife. His head kept telling his heart that he had no choice but to end the betrothal by divorce. It was the only proper thing for a decent man to do.

According to Jewish custom, the divorce could take place publicly before a court or privately with no more than two witnesses. He had no intention of exposing Mary to public disgrace, so he began thinking of candidates whom he might ask to witness the discreet ceremony of writing a divorce certificate at the synagogue. The man of honor and integrity would follow the requirements of the Law of Moses; the man of compassion and gentleness would nevertheless be sensitive to Mary.

With his mind finally settled about what must be done, Joseph was so exhausted that he quickly fell asleep. He would act tomorrow to settle the matter. For his sake and for hers, it would not be drawn out over a long period of time. Tonight he would rest his tortured heart with sleep.

As he slept, however, an angel of the Lord appeared to him in a dream. "Joseph son of David, do not be afraid to take Mary home as your wife, because what is conceived in her is from the Holy Spirit," the angel said. "She will give birth to a son, and you are to give him the name Jesus, because he will save his people from their sins" (Matt. 1:20-21).

When Joseph awakened, he had no doubt that his dream was a clear communication from Yahweh. He knew the Old Testament precedent of God speaking to men in dreams. He had never had such a dream before, but he had no reservation about accepting this as an authoritative word from God. Mary had told him the truth! How could he face her now? How could he tell her what he had intended to do tomorrow? Would she find it in her heart to forgive him? The tables were suddenly turned on Joseph!

He didn't have time to think about such things or to prepare a contrite speech for her. He had to find Mary. He had to tell her about his dream. He had to bring her home with him that very day—if she would come. He would not wait for the wedding feast that had been planned. He would make her his wife today. He would let the townspeople think whatever they would. He would obey the word from God, claim Mary as his wife, and protect the precious child she would bear.

Although it was still early in the day, Joseph rushed to Mary's home. He insisted on seeing her. "It is urgent," he insisted. "I must talk to her."

No one in Mary's family had ever seen Joseph so agitated and assertive about anything. Knowing that it must be important, they called for Mary. And the little girl who had been so frightened during the past few days of Joseph's silence was overwhelmed by his outpouring.

The words came in a torrent. He told of the dream. He described the angel and repeated the explanation he brought. He recounted the command. Then, compelled by his guilty conscience, he told what he had been thinking before the dream. But Mary stopped him.

"Shhh. Don't!" she pleaded. "How could you have believed without a sign? Your dream is another sign to me that the impossible is really happening! We will believe it together now. We will wait for more signs that God will surely give. We will wait for the birth of the baby. And God will be with us."

"And God will be with us," repeated Joseph.

9

SKELETONS IN THE CLOSET

Several years back, it was quite the rage. Everyone was tracing his or her family tree. Interest has dropped off now, however, and I may know why. Too many of us found too many undesirable relatives. We found skeletons in our closets! We turned up too many squirrels in our family trees.

The New Testament traces Jesus' family tree not once, but twice. And what a genealogy it is! It is filled with such notable figures as Abraham and Jacob, David and Solomon, Hezekiah and Josiah. But there are other names that startle us, the likes of which might cause some of us to call off the search for the identities of our ancestors.

Rehoboam (Matt. 1:7) was the foolish king so determined to begin his rule with a tough-guy image that he split the nation of Israel permanently into two groups (1 Kings 12:1ff).

Manasseh (Matt. 1:10) had this judgment passed on his fifty-five-year reign over Judah: "He has done more evil than the Amorites who preceded him and has led Judah into sin with his idols" (2 Kings 21:11b).

69

Unusual in the family tree of Jesus is the naming of four women, since Hebrew genealogies are typically traced through the males. Almost bizarre, however, is that *every* one of the four is somehow "tainted."

Tamar (Matt. 1:3), disguised as a prostitute, seduced her father-in-law into an incestuous liaison that led to the birth of twins (Gen. 38:6ff).

He came to save us all, including those with a tainted past, a family stigma, or a personal scandal.

Rahab (Matt. 1:5a) was a pagan woman who plied her trade as a prostitute in Jericho before the Israelites arrived and Yahweh destroyed it by a miracle (Josh. 2:1).

Ruth (Matt. 1:5b), a woman of noble character, was nevertheless a Moabite (Ruth 1:1-4). And the Moabites were among the people forbidden to enter "the assembly of the Lord" for ten generations (Deut. 23:3).

Finally, there is *Bathsheba* (Matt. 1:6b), the woman who committed adultery with King David while her husband was away on military duty (2 Sam. 11:1ff).

Why tell the complete story? Why include these names in Jesus' family tree? Because he came to save us all, including those with a tainted past, a family stigma, or a personal scandal hanging over our heads.

Jew and Gentile, male and female, distinguished and reprobate—everyone needs a Savior. In Jesus Christ, there is grace greater than your circumstance.

10
DID HE DO ENOUGH?

It had been a night the like of which Joseph had never dreamed could occur. Away from their home, their friends, and all familiar surroundings, his young wife had given birth to a son in a hillside cave. The place was ordinarily used to shelter animals on the outskirts of Bethlehem.

As Joseph looked at Mary, asleep now, he could not keep back the tears. He should have been able to provide something better for her tonight. They had just arrived in the city of David, and there had been no room in the overcrowded inns. That they had even this much sanctuary was due to a stranger's kindness rather than Joseph's ingenuity or ability to provide.

This precious woman who was "highly favored" (Luke 1:28) and "blessed among women" (Luke 1:42) had been entrusted to his care. But the best he had been able to do tonight was a cave, a tiny cleared area, and a bed of straw covered by his cloak. "I should have been able to do more for her," he whispered.

Then he looked at the baby. He was so incredibly tiny and helpless. He was totally dependent on a

Galilean carpenter and his teenage wife. How could it be! This was God's own son, not his. This baby was himself the God of creation, of Abraham, of Moses. Why, he was the God of Joseph and Mary! How could he be lying beside Mary now?

> *This baby was the God of Joseph and Mary. How could he be lying beside Mary now?*

Yet Joseph believed with all his heart what the angel had told him six months ago. This baby had been conceived by the Holy Spirit and would save people from their sins. "I should have been able to do better than this for him," said Joseph.

Then, on the verge of weeping aloud and waking both mother and baby, the devout man realized that his self-pity was born of pride rather than holiness. No angel had come to him tonight to say that he had done too little. He had had no dream. There had been no word of divine rebuke.

What has Israel's God ever required of anyone? Only that he do what is within his power. And Joseph had done that. He had obeyed Caesar in traveling to Bethlehem. He had protected Mary as best he could from the rigors of the trip. He had provided the only shelter available to them in the home city of his fathers. Was it now his duty to feel guilty that he could not do more?

Perhaps Joseph sensed at that moment what others of us need yet to learn: God is served best by the smallest of deeds done in love. It is faithfulness within the sphere of the possible that serves the divine will, not grandiose accomplishments.

Perhaps Joseph later told his foster son of his feelings of inadequacy. And maybe it was to counter such needless fears in us that Jesus later taught that anyone who can give a cup of cold water to a thirsty person, give shelter to homeless strangers, put clothes on a shivering child, or take time to visit a sick person is accounted as doing those things to him.

Was Joseph serving the Christ-child that night in ministering to him in an animal shelter? Do we serve him any less when we offer our ministries now? And would he want us to feel guilty that we cannot do more than use the resources he has placed in our hands? I've never done enough for God in any setting, but I'm beginning to understand that my incomplete and imperfect attempts are all he has ever asked.

A committed, loving heart served God's son at Bethlehem in the only way he could. The Father asks of us only what he asked of Joseph on that holy night.

ANGELS

11
THE HEAVENLY HOST

Angels in heaven may well have rejoiced to know that "the time had fully come." All of heaven swung into motion at a predetermined instant. It was time for the Word to become flesh, for the glory of the Beloved Son to be seen, and for sin's stranglehold on the human race to yield.

> Angels we have heard on high
>   Sweetly singing o'er the plains,
> And the mountains in reply
>   Echo back their joyous strains.

Gabriel at Nazareth may well have marveled at the faith of Mary. A mere child would give birth to a child. Engaged but not yet married, she embraced pain as well as glory. She believed in a God who can do impossible things, so she accepted an angel's word that she would conceive though a virgin. Her attitude at that moment was her attitude forever: "I am the Lord's servant."

Shepherds, why this jubilee?
  Why your joyous strains prolong?
Say what may the tidings be,
  Which inspire your heavenly song?

Angels may well have cringed for the confusion of Joseph as he paced his carpenter's shop. How was he supposed to know? Should he be expected to believe Mary without a sign of his own to confirm the greater sign? The angel sent to speak to him in a dream and take away his fears must have accepted the mission as a pleasant one.

Come to Bethlehem and see
  Him whose birth the angels sing;
Come adore, on bended knee,
  Christ, the Lord, the newborn King.

---

*Angels may well have
wept for the sacrifice
their Master had made.*

Angels hovering near Bethlehem on the night of his birth may well have giggled at the surprise written on the faces of shepherds tending their flocks. You'll have to admit that these men were unlikely choices to hear the first word of Messiah's birth. What must it have looked like from the angels' overhead vantage point? They surely saw big eyes, open mouths, and shaking knees. Shepherds were called to see the one who was destined to be the Lamb of God who takes away the sin of the world.

> Gloria in excelsis Deo,
>> Gloria in excelsis Deo.
> Glory to God in the highest,
>> Glory to God in the highest.

Angels, aware of their blessed state in heaven that night, may well have wept for the sacrifice their Master had made. He had stepped down from glory and was emptying himself. On that fateful night, he was born of woman and subjected to limitations beneath theirs. They saw it as the ultimate sacrifice. Little could they know how total the sacrifice would be before his Earth-visit was completed.

12
THEY'RE STILL WATCHING

All angels are "ministering spirits sent to serve those who will inherit salvation" (Heb. 1:14). They are spirit beings created by God long before the material universe was made. Perhaps they participated in its creation. At the very least, they "shouted for joy" as they watched God call all physical things into existence (Job 38:4-7).

The Bible indicates that there are thousands upon thousands of these heavenly creatures who surround the throne of God, adore and praise his holiness, and stand ready to do his will. Since most of the Old Testament references to angels are found in the Prophets rather than in the Torah, the Sadducees rejected the doctrine of angels (Acts 23:8). The Pharisees, by contrast, not only accepted their existence but also developed an extensive angelology.

Most often in Scripture, angels become involved in human affairs as the means of communicating important messages from heaven to earth. Thus they appeared to such characters as Abraham (Gen. 18:1-16), Gideon (Judg. 6:11ff), and others. Perhaps because of their involvement in ministry to God's people on earth, they seem to have an intense interest in human beings. Peter, for example, wrote of the prophetic messages given to men of long ago—with many of them mediated through angels—and observed that angels were always curious to find out the meaning of those utterances (1 Pet. 1:10-12).

Even though thousands of these heavenly beings exist, only two (unless one includes Satan, the angel who fell from his high estate) are named in the Bible. One of them is Michael (Dan. 10:13, 21; 12:1; Jude 9; Rev. 12:7), and the other is Gabriel. Along with Michael, Gabriel was involved in the events of the life of Daniel (Dan. 8:16; 9:21), but Gabriel's most dramatic moments in the biblical record came in connection with the events surrounding the birth of Jesus.

Do angels volunteer for missions? Or is everything by assignment? If their work is done by assignment, as I suspect it is, was Gabriel chosen to work in the birth of the Son of God because of an especially intense desire for the salvation of his fleshly cousins? Or was it just a quirk of fate? If those were the exhaustive options, I know which I would select.

Angels apparently have some knowledge of our fallenness and the pain sin brings to our lives. Perhaps because they know the fate of some of their own fellow angels who sinned, were cast out of heaven, and are destined to hell forever (Matt. 25:41), they are grieved for the lost of Earth. Perhaps because their own joy in heaven is so complete, they are unselfishly eager that we should participate in that same fullness of joy.

Do angels experience an emotion comparable to human anxiety? Did Gabriel carry a burden in his heart from the time he saw creation turn from its original perfection? What might he have felt if he witnessed the rebellion of Eve and Adam? What would he have thought about the murmuring and unbelief of ancient Israel in the wilderness? Did he turn away in despair from the continual apostasies of humanity during the period of the prophets? Perhaps he assumed the cause of human redemption was hopeless when the prophetic period came to a close and revelation from the throne ceased to be ferried to mortals.

Did Gabriel carry a burden in his heart from the time he saw creation turn from its original perection?

In a moment of freedom from whatever responsibilities he had, the plight of humans might have crossed Gabriel's mind one day. Walking down a golden street, basking in the eternal light that bathes heaven constantly, perhaps he remembered that men and women were plodding the earth in spiritual darkness. How long had it been since anyone had been sent from here to there? As best he could calculate human time measurements, it must have been about four hundred years ago. And Gabriel's worst fear was that nobody down there had even noticed the silence. Perhaps no one on Earth even cared any more.

Then a call came from the throne. Yahweh was summoning Gabriel. Without so much as a millisecond's delay, he was standing in the immediate presence of the Ancient of Days.

"Gabriel," said a voice from the throne. And the angel, who was accustomed to face-to-face conversations with deity, marveled all over again at the sound of that voice. It carried simultaneously the authority that could call a universe into existence by uttering one word and the tenderness that could make one know that he was valued beyond any worth of his own.

"Gabriel, the time is right for us to break our silence. The precise moment we have been waiting for has come. We are going to speak to Earth one last time. The WORD will go forth to men. In fact, the WORD will become flesh and live for a while among humankind. This is our last chance—and theirs."

There is no evidence in Scripture that suggests angels have immediate insight into divine mysteries. In fact, all the evidence is against it. They did not understand the meaning of the prophecies they helped give to men in the days of Moses, Isaiah, or Micah. So how could Gabriel understand the means of their fulfillment?

The WORD will leave heaven? The WORD will live in flesh? The WORD will become human? How can it be?

Because it is his nature to be gracious, Yahweh may have proceeded at that point to clear away the confusion. As Jesus would later do with the disciples after his resurrection, perhaps now some member of the Godhead opened Gabriel's mind to understand what had been foretold and how it would be fulfilled (cf. Luke 24:45). Perhaps the entire heavenly host was informed of what was about to happen and was put on alert for various roles to be carried out in the divine drama.

> *The angels ministering before the heavenly throne would be obedient and follow the schedule.*

If the significance of these events was explained to him, one can almost imagine the excitement Gabriel felt about being chosen to bear the glad news to earth. He was to announce the birth of John to Zechariah and the birth of Jesus to Mary. But there was a timetable. Nothing could be rushed. The events would happen at precisely the time God had determined. Nothing would happen a moment too soon. Nothing would happen an instant too late.

Gabriel and the other angels ministering before the heavenly throne would be obedient and follow the schedule. Yet they wondered why Joseph would learn about the baby so much later than Mary. Might that confuse Joseph? Would he believe Mary's report? If so, why would an angel need to explain anything to him? But these issues were not for angels to resolve. They would simply obey, follow the timetable that had been worked out, and believe that God would unfold his purposes.

The day came for Gabriel to go to Zechariah. The angel knew him. He was an upright man, a priest belonging to the Abijah division. He and his wife, Elizabeth, had prayed for a child during all the years of their long and happy marriage, but Elizabeth was barren. Now that they were both past the age of having children, they had accepted their fate. They were local favorites with the children near their home in the hill country of Judea, everybody's Aunt Elizabeth and Uncle Zechariah. Their obvious love for children had made many people comment on the pity it was that they could never have children of their own.

Zechariah was on duty at the temple in Jerusalem on the day Gabriel went to him. At the moment of his appearing, the old priest was placing incense on the altar inside the Holy Place of the temple. Whether Gabriel appeared as a full-blown angel, wings and all, or simply as a man isn't told in the record. In either case, Zechariah would have been startled because this part of the temple was off-limits to anyone except the priests on duty.

When Zechariah saw him, he was startled and seized with fear. Gabriel spoke and said to him, "Do not be afraid, Zechariah; your prayer has been heard. Your wife Elizabeth will bear you a son, and you are to give him the name John. He will be a joy and delight to you, and many will rejoice because of his birth, for he will be great in the sight of the Lord. He is never to take wine or other fermented drink, and he will be filled with the Holy Spirit even from birth. Many of the people of Israel will he bring back to the Lord their God. And he will go on before the Lord, in the spirit and power of Elijah, to turn the hearts of the fathers to their children and the disobedient to the wisdom of the righteous—to make ready a people prepared for the Lord" (Luke 1:13-17).

Gabriel saw the look on Zechariah's wrinkled face, a mixture of excitement and incredulity. He thought that he had probably put a strain on the elderly man's heart by giving him such news!

Then Zechariah spoke to him and asked, "How can I be sure of this? I am an old man and my wife is well along in years."

The angel was neither rebuffed nor angered by the priest's question. It was perfectly normal for a man his age to think it impossible that he would father a child by a wife who had been barren for all the years of their life together. This contingency had been anticipated and prepared for in the plan that Gabriel had been given.

So the angel spoke again and said, "I am Gabriel. I stand in the presence of God, and I have been sent to speak to you and to tell you this good news. And now you will be silent and not able to speak until the day this happens, because you did not believe my words, which will come true at their proper time."

Gabriel smiled at his words to Zechariah about things coming true at their proper time. He had wondered about things happening on Earth, but now he knew that God had a plan and was carrying it out. Soon Zechariah would know it, too.

Meanwhile, people outside the temple were wondering what was taking Zechariah so long. Then, when he did come out, he was unable to speak. The best he could do was make signs with his hands and try to communicate by the gestures he made. Later someone would suggest that he write down what he wanted to say.

He made them understand that he had seen a vision, but he was both unable and unwilling to share its content. It was a matter to be shared first with his wife, Elizabeth.

When he had finished his period of service at the temple, for his inability to speak did not keep him from his work, he hurried to his home. At first, Elizabeth was frightened when her husband was unable to speak. But as he communicated through the slow, painful process of signs and written notes, she understood and believed. And she became pregnant.

Gabriel watched all this with eager interest. The plan of God was unfolding. Everything was happening right on time.

When Elizabeth was in the sixth month of her pregnancy, Gabriel was dispatched again. This time he was sent to Nazareth, a town in Galilee, to a virgin named Mary. The announcement he took her was even more startling than the one he had carried to Zechariah. Old people such as Abraham had been enabled by God to have children before. But his message to Mary was that she would conceive a child without losing her virginity!

He appeared to her in her house, saying, "Greetings, you who are highly favored! The Lord is with you." As he spoke the words, he saw the same look of fear on her face that he had seen on Zechariah's a few months before. But this face was different. It was so beautiful. It was so young. It was utterly innocent and trusting.

He said, "Do not be afraid, Mary, you have found favor with God. You will be with child and give birth to a son, and you are to call his name Jesus. He will be great and will be called the Son of the Most High. The Lord God will give him the throne of his father David, and he will reign over the house of Jacob forever; his kingdom will never end" (Luke 1:30-33).

Gabriel remembered the promises to David, some of which he had helped deliver. Now he knew what they meant! The eternal WORD, soon to live in human form, was about to fulfill them. And Gabriel was standing before the woman who would provide the divine being he knew in heaven with the body he would have on Earth.

Mary spoke to ask, "How can this be, since I am a virgin?"

He answered, "The Holy Spirit will come upon you, and the power of the Most High will overshadow you. So the holy one to be born will be called the Son of God. Even Elizabeth your relative is going to have a child in her old age, and she who was said to be barren is in her sixth month. For nothing is impossible with God."

Then Gabriel saw a look of serene acceptance come over Mary's face as she said, "I am the Lord's servant. May it be to me as you have said" (Luke 1:34-38).

Gabriel was so moved by her statement of faith that he was speechless. He left her alone with her thoughts. And he was alone with his. It had been a long, long time since he had seen such faith. Only a few, rare people in history had been like Mary. Not one of those saints from ancient days had been just a child. It made the scene all the more incredible as Gabriel reflected on it.

Perhaps he determined at that instant to volunteer as Mary's personal guardian angel from that time forward. How he would cherish the honor of that assignment! He would see that no harm came to her from people who would not believe her story, that her trip to see Elizabeth was made safely, and that her pregnancy went smoothly. It is not hard to imagine that he returned to the throne room and asked permission to see this situation through for Mary's sake. It is not far-fetched in the least to think that Gabriel went around heaven telling other angels of the great faith of a teenage girl he had seen at Nazareth. Even an angel was probably at a loss for words to describe what he saw in her face.

Then three months later, Mary had a wonderful visit with her cousin Elizabeth, and they shared with each other the stories of their pregnancies. Each reinforced the faith of the other. On the eve of Elizabeth's delivery of her child, Mary returned home.

Gabriel watched over her trip and sensed Mary's growing anxiety as she drew nearer to Nazareth. She would have to face Joseph soon, tell him about the child she was carrying, and ask him to believe what an angel had told her about the baby's identity. The face that was so beautiful and serene began to show signs of tension. Gabriel may have wished he could handle the task for her and go directly to Joseph himself. When he checked the divine timetable, however, he discovered that Mary was to break the news to him. No angel could relieve her of the painful responsibility.

On God's timetable, an angel was to see Joseph in a dream. Whether Gabriel or another angel went to Joseph is unclear. The biblical text merely says that "an angel of the Lord appeared to him in a dream."

Even an angel was probably at a loss for words to describe what he saw in her face.

At the appointed time the angel of God came near the sleeping carpenter. He saw a face that was deeply tormented. Joseph was sleeping fitfully, tossing on his bed. The visiting angel could have seen the tracks of tears on both his cheeks if he had chosen to look closely, for Joseph had not accepted Mary's explanation. He was in anguish over the situation.

"Joseph son of David, do not be afraid to take Mary home as your wife, because what is conceived in her is from the Holy Spirit," said the angel. "She will give birth to a son, and you are to give him the name Jesus, because he will save his people from their sins" (John 1:20b-21).

Joseph's face lost its contorted look. He did not wake up, but he was now at peace in his sleep. His breathing was less anguished. He lay still. The angel who had borne the message may have felt a special sense of joy in the task performed, for it obviously had made an immediate and profound impact on Joseph to learn that the woman he loved was all that he had once thought she was. Mary was pure and chaste, so utterly devoted to God that she would risk both her wedding and her reputation for him. And now Joseph knew what his responsibility to her was.

As the angel left Joseph to his sleep, he may have reflected on a prophecy that had been given seven hundred years earlier through Isaiah and whose meaning had been discussed among the heavenly host from that time: "The virgin will be with child and will give birth to a son, and they will call him Immanuel."

The final event surrounding the birth of Jesus in which angels are specifically mentioned is their appearance to shepherds near Bethlehem on the night of the baby's birth. If there was ever the possibility of a group portrait of angels taken from an earthly perspective, surely it was on that night! One angel, perhaps Gabriel, got to make the revelation to the shepherds as they watched their flocks. "Do not be afraid. I bring you good news of great joy that will be for all the people. Today in the town of David a Savior has been born to you; he is Christ the Lord. This will be a sign to you: You will find a baby wrapped in strips of cloth and lying in a manger."

Then, as if every angel in heaven wanted to be involved in the event, "a great company of the heavenly host" joined that angel to praise God and to proclaim, "Glory to God in the highest, and on earth peace to men on whom his favor rests" (Luke 2:10-14).

It must have looked like a family photograph on July 4. Everybody wanted to be in the picture. Everybody crowded in close. Everybody smiled. It was an event to be remembered!

But can you imagine what it must have looked like from the perspective of the angels? Shepherds huddled around a hillside fire to fight off the night chill were startled by the appearance of one angel. But to be confronted by "a great company of the heavenly host" must have been more than a little unnerving. If angels have a hard time keeping straight faces when they see something funny, the whole group had to fight off laughter that night.

In spite of their dirty, smelly clothes, that group of shepherds was impressive in faith. When the angels disappeared from view, they immediately left to find the baby who had been born in Bethlehem that day. And they adored in a manger the eternal WORD whom the angels had worshipped and adored in heaven from the time he created them.

Angels. The word may cause you to think of winged beings on the far side of the universe, divorced from and uninterested in the human plight. But the involvement of angels in the coming of the Son of God to Earth serves notice to a very different relationship.

Ministering spirits, concerned observers, faithful messengers, anxious for our salvation—they are still watching today.

SHEPHERDS

13
SHEPHERDS WATCHING THEIR FLOCKS

As he sat with his fellow shepherds that night, he was alone with his thoughts. He was a conscientious, hard-working man. He was both honest and God-fearing. He was a good shepherd. It bothered him that some people looked at him as they did and assigned him such a bad name.

Shepherding had not always been so hard on one's self-esteem. It had always been hard work, but only recently had it become despised work. It was difficult for him to understand as he sat near the small hillside fire he and his partners had built that night.

The testimony of shepherds was not accepted in formal proceedings of Jewish courts. On the Sabbath, they could not enter the synagogue owing to the ceremonial uncleanness attached to them because of their work. It didn't seem fair to him that all shepherds should be lumped together, condemned collectively, and effectively left outside the community of Israel.

If people would only remember, King David had been a shepherd in his youth. Out of that experience, he wrote a beautiful psalm in which Yahweh is pictured as the shepherd of his people.

> The Lord is my shepherd, I shall not be in want.
>   He makes me lie down in green pastures,
> he leads me beside quiet waters,
>   he restores my soul.

It had always been hard work, but only recently had it become despised work.

This shepherd understood the imagery well. A shepherd who really cared for his sheep would move them periodically to locate the best grazing. Knowing that sheep are frightened by fast-moving water, he would seek out a place where the water was fresh but quiet enough for them to drink without fear. All day long—whether feeding them, watering them, driving them, or resting them—he would call their names, sing to them, and touch them. The sheep knew their owner, and it both reassured and refreshed them to be treated so tenderly by him.

> He guides me in paths of righteousness
>   for his name's sake.
> Even though I walk
>   through the valley of the shadow of death,
> I will fear no evil,

for you are with me;
  your rod and your staff,
    they comfort me.

He knew about choosing a secure path for his sheep. It needed to be clearly marked and as non-threatening as possible. He would talk aloud as he led his flock and allow his familiar voice to show the direction the sheep were to go. And if the sun were to set quickly and make the trip back to the fold a bit scary with its dimming light and long shadows, he would move the flock along with the reassuring touch of his rod and staff. His closeness seemed to reassure the sheep that no harm would come to them.

You prepare a table before me
  in the presence of my enemies.
You anoint my head with oil;
  my cup overflows.
Surely goodness and love will follow me
  all the days of my life,
and I will dwell in the house of the Lord
  forever.

Even if wild dogs or other predators should be nearby, a good shepherd would see that the sheep were fed at the end of the day. More than that, he would inspect each for cuts or wounds and pour soothing oil on any injury he found. The sheep would be sheltered in safety, for a good shepherd would risk his own life before he would let harm come to the sheep in his care.

101

Perhaps the fact that so many shepherds had themselves lost the vision of this noble work accounted for the bad image of his profession. With his family's long history of shepherding, though, he had been taught to take a higher view of the work than most of the hired workers seemed to have.

The hirelings were farmers forced to do something else by hard times, or craftsmen who had not been successful at their carpentry or masonry. Some of them didn't care about the sheep in their charge. Some were dishonest and had to be watched at any common grazing period lest they leave with one or two more sheep than they had had at the start of the day. This good man hated that he had to bear the image of those few.

Strange as it might sound, it even occurred to him that night that the association of so many shepherds around Bethlehem with the Jerusalem priests might be responsible for their bad image. Most of the Bethlehem shepherds sold lambs each spring to the priests, who then sold them in the temple marketplace as animals for sacrifice. He had seen some things in Jerusalem at festival time—bazaar-type hawking of animals around the temple and price gouging by the men handling animals—that offended him greatly. But how could the people feel that *he* had any part in that? He deplored turning a place of worship into a carnival as much as any devout man of Israel.

Why were all these thoughts rushing in on him tonight? They were making him melancholy on a beautiful night.

His flock was already settled for the night. He wished he could banish these brooding thoughts from his mind so he could enjoy the clear evening. He needed some sleep, too, for he would have to take his turn at watch in the middle of the night.

Then he heard something from the direction of his sheepfold. Was a predator near? What was disturbing his sheep? He moved to them quickly and discovered the problem in an instant. A ewe was giving birth. By the time he arrived, she had already dropped her lamb. There had been no bleating or crying. It is simply not in the nature of sheep, it appears, to thrash about and make noise. They have an amazing restraint and meekness about them.

As the shepherd watched the mother nuzzle and clean her lamb, he saw that it was a male. And he thought to himself that within a year it would likely be offered in sacrifice to the Lord on the Jerusalem altar. As a shepherd whose task it was to present such lambs ready for sacrifice, he would take care to see that this lamb was spotless and without blemish. Only a flawless lamb was proper to be offered to the Lord.

Back at the fire, he was torn between conflicting feelings. On the one hand, there was the matter of his image as a shepherd. On the other hand, there was the issue of God's choice of the shepherd image to represent his own relationship to Israel. Is a shepherd's lot to suffer indignities or to give glory to God? Can anyone who is despised and rejected of men be close to the heart of God? He thought for a moment about sharing his meditations with the other shepherds crouched near the fire beside him. But, no. It was time to rest. No need to talk about irresolvable conjectures. Maybe things like this would be made plain with the arrival of Messiah.

Suddenly he and his fellow shepherds were startled by a brilliant light shining around them. No, "startled" is not a strong enough word. They were terrified. Some of them fell to their knees, others were frozen on their feet or in their typical crouching posture near the fire. He had never seen anything like it before. It was like the sun shining at midday. He was too frightened to run and too confused to speak. What was happening?

Then he heard a voice. It was not one of the other shepherds, whose voices he knew well. In fact, the voice was not coming from their direction. It was coming from above, from the direction of the light. Shielding his eyes as he lifted his head, he looked in the direction of the voice and saw what was unquestionably an angel. The angel was saying, "Do not be afraid. I bring you good news of great joy that will be for all the people. Today in the town of David a Savior has been born to you; he is Christ the Lord" (Luke 2:10-11).

Was the whole world hearing this news simultaneously? Surely he and his shepherd friends were not being singled out to receive this announcement! Would God reveal the most wonderful news the world had ever heard to men whom others held in contempt? Was the coming of the divine Messiah announced to shepherds before it was told to priests?

Did the angel say that the Savior-Messiah had been "born" today? Could the Lord's anointed be coming into the world in so humble a way? And why would it be happening at Bethlehem rather than in Jerusalem? Was his hearing failing? Was his mind playing tricks? No, for the angel continued, "This will be a sign to you: You will find a baby wrapped in strips of cloth and lying in a manger" (Luke 2:12).

A sign indeed! The "sign" was not that a baby would be wrapped in long strips of cloth to keep him warm. Every child born to a Jewish mother of that time was warmed and protected with swaddling clothes at birth. The "sign" was that this child—divine, the Savior, the Messiah—should be found lying in a manger. A manger is a feeding trough for animals! Usually cut into the rock walls of a cave or made of wood if the sheepfold was outdoors, a manger was no place for such a precious child to be laid on the day of his birth. Had there been no other place for him? More incredible still, had he somehow suffered a rejection at his birth? Was that why the announcement of his birth was being made to people who were outcasts themselves?

Then, startling the shepherds all over again, a great company of other angels appeared with the one who had spoken. They joined together and, as with one voice, sang, "Glory to God in the highest, and on earth peace to men on whom his favor rests" (Luke 2:14).

As quickly as they had appeared, the angels left the shepherds and vanished from view. The light faded. The night was still again.

No one dared to break the stillness. The moment had to be savored and kept in memory. Then, as if on cue, the silence was interrupted. Every shepherd spoke to every other and said the same thing: "Let's go to Bethlehem and see this thing that has happened, which the Lord has told us about" (Luke 2:15b).

They hurried into Bethlehem, leaving the animals to their sleep in the middle of the night. From what the angels had said, they knew that the child most likely had not been born to a family native to the town. Otherwise why would the baby be in a manger? So they asked at public places about new people who were in town.

They especially wanted to know about any woman who was expecting a child. Some people treated them rudely, others did not reply at all. Finally, a kindly innkeeper told them that he had seen a couple earlier that night, that the woman was indeed pregnant, and that he had offered them his stable for the night because there was no room in his inn.

The shepherds looked at one another with an instinctive awareness that they had found the child. They moved in the direction the innkeeper had pointed. Cautiously and reverently, they moved near the mouth of the cave. Could this be the place? There were no crowds, no heavenly lights, no angels in chorus. Would God show this special child to these men alone on the night of his birth?

One of them called, and an exhausted-looking man appeared. He identified himself as Joseph, explaining that he was there by permission. He appeared frightened that the newcomers might evict him and take back the space for themselves. He explained that he had just reached the city from Nazareth. He was not sure whether to say anything about Mary and the baby.

The shepherds interrupted to allay his fears. They were not there to reclaim the shelter for their animals. They were not there to kick Joseph out. They were seeking the Christ-child, the Messiah, for an angel had told them that he had been born today in Bethlehem and would be found lying in a manger.

Tears ran down his cheeks as he fell to his knees in worship.

Joseph excused himself to tell his wife that the men were waiting outside. Then he returned, called them in, and asked that they repeat for Mary what had just happened to them. For the moment, however, they said nothing. They moved near the manger, standing so that the dim light of the cave shone on the baby's face.

The shepherd who had only a couple of hours ago seen a newborn lamb looked now at the newborn Savior-Messiah of Israel. Tears ran down his cheeks as he fell to his knees in worship.

Little could he know that he was looking at the one who was destined to be The Good Shepherd who would lay down his own life for God's flock. This child was born to be the Lamb of God who had come to take away the sins of the world. He would come to Jerusalem years hence to offer himself as God's ultimate Passover Lamb. In that act, he would make all previous sacrifices of lambs meaningful—and all future sacrifices unnecessary.

14
GOD COMES TO UNLIKELY PEOPLE

Have you ever noticed how God makes himself known to people? There is no consistency as to place or time. It happens on mountain tops, at the Jerusalem temple, and in prison cells. The communication comes by dreams, in visions, or through spoken words.

The most consistent thing I have noticed about his revelations has to do with the people selected for them. They tend to be the most unlikely of choices for coming into contact with deity. Moses was a criminal fleeing Egyptian authorities. Amos was a farmer going about his work. Peter was a fisherman on the lake. Paul was an avowed enemy of the church on his way to put Christians in prison.

Did ever so unlikely a group of people receive a divine revelation as when shepherds tending their flocks were called to the birthplace of the Son of God? If you had been in charge of making the announcement, whom would you have invited? Kings, clergy, and prominent citizens would make most lists. Chances are that you would never have thought of shepherds to the exclusion of all others on the night of his appearance. No public-relations firm worth its salt would have come up with this plan.

Shepherds who lived in the fields with their animals smelled no better than the animals themselves. As a group, they had a bad reputation. They were known for "confusing" sheep as they moved from one grassy spot to another. Shepherds were considered so unreliable that they were not permitted to testify in law courts among their own people.

> *Shepherds who lived in the fields with their animals smelled no better than the animals themselves.*

But God wanted shepherds nearest to his son on the night of his birth. It was as if their presence was meant to signify that God would, from now on, be nearest to the people others despised. He declared himself that night to be not only the Lord Almighty, but also the God of the Outcasts. True to that image, the babe adored by shepherds grew up to be called Friend of Tax Collectors and Sinners. It was meant to be derision. I understand it as my basis for hope of eternal life.

If you were charged with choosing a handful of people to see heaven come down to earth, would you pick a group that included you? "It isn't likely!" you say. "And neither would anyone else pick me." You have just placed yourself in the very class of people to whom God has most consistently revealed himself. You are the most likely of candidates on God's list.

With all your hang-ups, problems, and quirks, God loves you. In spite of the alcohol, divorce, or poverty, you are made in his image. No matter that you have doubts, a criminal record, or a prodigal child, God seeks to reveal himself to you. Whether you can read well, know the name of your child's father, or think that the world would be better off if you had never been born, you need to be aware that God comes to just such people as yourself.

How would you describe this phenomenon of God's tendency to seek out the most unlikely of people? Perhaps your word of choice is strange. The one that occurs to me is *wonderful*.

DEVOUT SEEKERS

15
WATCHING THE TEMPLE PRECINCTS

The birth of a child was typically a festive occasion in Israel. In connection with the birth of boys in particular, family friends and guests would often gather every night for seven days to celebrate what became known as "son's week." Then, on the eighth day, there would be a celebration with feasting in connection with the circumcision of the baby.

The covenant of circumcision traces back to Abraham. When the Father of the Faithful was ninety-nine years old, Yahweh made an "everlasting covenant" with him and his descendants: God would multiply his offspring, give them a special land to possess, and through that nation bring the Messiah into the world. The sign of that covenant was the circumcision of every male born to Abraham's offspring. "For the generations to come," he was told, "every male among you who is eight days old must be circumcised" (Gen. 17:1-14).

Whereas several cultures practiced circumcision as a puberty rite to signify status as an adult, the nation of

Israel was charged to practice it as a sign of covenant commitment and personal consecration to Yahweh. As with every symbolic act among the Jews, the blood associated with the rite was especially meaningful. It pointed to the costliness of responding to the divine call. One who has been called to covenant relationship with the Lord has accepted a demand that involves his blood, his life, his total being.

---

*His presence would
bring people to a point
of decision.*

Joseph and Mary received their son with great personal rejoicing. Scripture always regards Jesus as Joseph's son as well as Mary's, though it is understood always that he is the son of Joseph by law and custom rather than by conception. The happy parents shared their joy with the shepherds sent to them on the night of his birth. What happened during the remainder of the week, we do not know.

Since the birth of the child meant that additional time would have to be spent at Bethlehem, some of that week would have been spent in finding better lodging for the family. Perhaps there was time for Joseph to find kinspeople in the town with whom to share a son's week. Perhaps they spent the week together in private contemplation of all that had happened. Perhaps the shepherds returned again and

again with people of their own kind who either believed or wanted to see for themselves what had been
reported about this family from Nazareth. Perhaps
God sent other people, as he had sent the shepherds,
to see the baby during his first week of life. Scripture is
silent about the events from the night of his birth until
the eighth day following it.

Devout as they were, Joseph and Mary had known
that their son would be circumcised at the appropriate
time. So, on the eighth day, the operation was done.

The custom was that the time of circumcision was
also the time of formal naming. So, just as John had
been named by Zechariah and Elizabeth on the eighth
day following his birth (Luke 1:59-66), Jesus was
named on the eighth day of his life. Joseph and Mary
watched as a Levite surgeon, who was a stranger to
them, performed the operation. Then Joseph stepped
forward to speak the name that had been given by the
angel before the child had been conceived. He may
have used the same words that the angel had spoken
to him: "You are to give him the name Jesus" (Matt.
1:21).

The Law of Moses required that firstborn sons be
redeemed and that mothers be purified after childbirth.
Ideally, both these rites were to take place at the temple in Jerusalem. Thus, sometime before the one-
month anniversary of the birth of Jesus, the little family
completed its registration with the Bethlehem census
officials and made a six-mile journey to Jerusalem.

On the night of the last plague before the Exodus,
the firstborn sons of the Egyptians had died. By virtue
of slaying a passover lamb and placing its blood around

the doors of the homes of the Israelites, their firstborn sons were spared. On that night Yahweh commanded, "Redeem every firstborn among your sons" (Exod. 13:13b). Later, in giving the details of this procedure through Moses, he said, "When they are a month old, you must redeem them at the redemption price set at five shekels of silver" (Num. 18:16a).

Because of the sacredness of blood in the Mosaic system, women had to undergo a ceremony of purification forty days after the birth of a son or seventy-three days after the birth of a daughter. The mother was under obligation to offer a lamb in sacrifice or, if she was too poor to bring a lamb, two doves or two young pigeons (Lev. 12:6-8).

And so it was that Joseph and Mary came to be in Jerusalem with the baby. One can hardly imagine how they must have felt to be in the temple courts. Bringing with them the child who was born to be the Savior of his people from their sins, they must have walked the compound as many hours per day as Mary's strength would allow. They would alternately listen to a rabbi teach or join in times of prayer or watch various rituals being performed. All the while, they were carrying history's greatest secret in their hearts. Neither priests nor Levites nor worshippers such as themselves had reason to know the identity of their son.

Or did someone there know? God had revealed it to shepherds at Bethlehem, hadn't he? Surely the idea crossed their minds at some point that it may have been—or might yet be—made known to someone in Jerusalem. They received polite smiles from people who saw them with their baby. Some may have asked to see him, to know his age, or to hear his name. Then, at some point in their stay at Jerusalem, they encountered Simeon and Anna.

Simeon was a righteous and devout man who was awaiting the arrival of Israel's Messiah and the consolation he would bring to Yahweh's people. More than that, he had been given a prophetic word from the Holy Spirit that he would see the Lord's Christ before he died.

One morning Simeon felt a distinct and clear prompting to go to the temple courts. Without resisting the Spirit of God, he went, not knowing what was to happen. Then a couple carrying a baby caught his eye.

Joseph and Mary were making their way toward the area where sons were presented before the Lord and redeemed with five shekels of silver. Although it must have represented a large percentage of their total estate—for later they would not have the thirty shekels needed to buy a lamb for Mary's purification and would offer the sacrifice of the poor, two birds—it would never have crossed their minds to begrudge the money.

As they walked with a solemnity appropriate to their purpose, Joseph and Mary were startled by Simeon. Yet, in view of the things that had happened in their lives of late, they did not resist him.

Moved both to act and to speak by the Holy Spirit, Simeon took the baby Jesus into his own arms. He spoke with a spirit of prophecy and said,

Sovereign Lord, as you have promised,
  you now dismiss your servant in peace.
For my eyes have seen your salvation,
  which you have prepared in the sight of all
    people,
a light for revelation to the Gentiles
  and for glory to your people Israel. (Luke 2:29-32)

Joseph and Mary marveled at what he said. Yes, they knew already that Jesus was destined to be the Savior. But he was to be the redeemer of Gentiles as well as of Israel?

They had no time to think now about the meaning of his opening words, for he was speaking still. He was not speaking of the baby now, but to them. He blessed them both. Then he turned to Mary and said, "This child is destined to cause the falling and rising of many in Israel, and to be a sign that will be spoken against, so that the thoughts of many hearts will be revealed" (Luke 2:34-35).

Their minds struggled to keep pace with his words. Yes, the presence of God's salvation would surely reveal the hearts of men. Those who loved the Lord and were eager to receive his salvation would welcome this child, as Simeon had done. His presence would bring people to a point of decision.

But Simeon may have introduced a new dimension to the growing knowledge Joseph and Mary had of this child's fate. His presence would be a sign "spoken against"? Would he suffer hostility at the hands of the enemies of God? Would unbelievers not only reject him but actively oppose him? Would he in any sense be vulnerable before those destined to fall in Israel because of his appearing?

Then Mary heard Simeon's final words: "And a sword will pierce your own soul too." Mary's heart had already been broken by some people at Nazareth, by their whispered gossip and their treatment of Joseph. Was there something even worse ahead?

Then, with her mother's heart, she realized that it would be more painful to see her son mistreated than to suffer mistreatment herself. But what would that cruel treatment involve? Verbal abuse? Simeon had said a "sword" would pierce her soul. Her soul *also*. Would she and her son be pursued by violent people? Would the two of them die at the hands of evil men? Was that the meaning of Simeon's prophecy? She would willingly die for her son. That he should have to die on her account was unthinkable! No, let others die for him. But don't let him have to die for others!

As Simeon was speaking, a fifth person joined the group and also began to speak. The woman was Anna, the daughter of Phanuel, of the tribe of Asher. Eighty-four years old, she spent every day in the temple precincts. Fasting and praying constantly, she also had the gift of prophecy. Hearing Simeon's identification of this child as the promised salvation from above, she confirmed it with her own prophetic power. She praised God for the child. Afterward, she spoke about the baby to other devout people who were looking forward to the redemption of Jerusalem as a center for true worship to the Lord (Luke 2:36-38).

Unlike the shepherds who were going about the routine of their lives only to have God break in unexpectedly, Simeon and Anna represent that host of people in every generation who look for God in the most likely of places only to find him in the most unlikely of persons. They hovered in the temple precincts, but they did not find God through the musicians, singers, Levites, or priests. They found him in a peasant child who was brought there by his nondescript parents.

Because they were looking for God in sincerity and because of God's promise that he would appear to them, they recognized him when he came. And they received him with joy.

The person who wills to know the truth will not have it hidden from him.

Our world also contains millions of devout people who are actively seeking God. Because they believe it is the place where God should be sought, they go to church. But most who ever find him there do not do so through musicians, preachers, or writers. They find him in the lives of humble people who serve God without fanfare or notice. They are salt-of-the-earth people, light-of-the-world types. People who are cynical about preachers or suspicious of having their emotions manipulated by music cease to resist God's presence in their lives when one person notices, cares, and models the truth of God before them.

God is faithful. The person who wills to know the truth will not have it hidden from him. That devout, seeking heart will be satisfied. But the satisfaction may come through unexpected persons.

That person may be the one who has loved you enough to listen, to phone you last week, or to remind you of Christ's forgiving nature when you were mad at someone yesterday. Maybe it was the one who wrote a note of encouragement. Perhaps it was the one who walked up beside you last Sunday, hugged you, and said, "I'm glad you're here today. I was looking for you."

Or, just perhaps, you may be that person for someone else today.

16
WHO WILL RECOGNIZE GOD'S SON?

When the God who made the world came into it, the world did not recognize him. When he came to be the world's true light, the world shut its eyes against him. When he came to his own, his own would not receive him.

The *humanists* of his time had so secularized religion that it was impotent and tasteless. They were skeptical and worldly. They were embarrassed by the notion of angels or a resurrection of the dead. The supernatural had given way to the practical, explainable, repeatable, and non-prophetic. They could not see God. They were called Sadducees.

The *clergy* of Jesus' day had so professionalized religion that they had taken it away from the people who looked to them to reveal God. They were aloof and abstract in their teaching. They cloistered themselves in their studies. When they spoke, they were dry and irrelevant to life. Erudite, scholarly, and distinguished looking, but lacking the fire of God and distant from hurting people. They could neither see God themselves nor show him to others. They were the scribes and priests.

The *hypocrites* of his time—and every generation has its share of them—had externalized religion, making it into forms, rituals, and ceremonies. They took the heart out of religion by taking their hearts out of religion. Holy days, holy places, holy words: these meant everything. Holy living meant nothing. They walked right by God, pausing only to sneer at him. Many people of this type were members of the party of the Pharisees.

They were prepared to leave the old in order to be part of the Messiah's new age.

The *nationalists* of his day had identified God with country and had turned religion into racial bigotry and exclusivism. They were so sure that God was on their side that they took no thought about being sure they were on God's side. Whatever advanced the interests of the state was judged holy. Lying, breaking treaties, tolerating scandals among their leaders—these unholy things were deemed "standard operating procedure." They knew God only to use his name for oaths and curses. They were called Zealots.

The people who had kept faith alive in Israel were not known by a party label. They were often frightened for the nation by the hawkish talk of the Zealots. They were embarrassed both by the pretensions of the Pharisees and the unbelief of the Sadducees. And they never would have attempted to argue theology with a priest or scribe.

These people were obscure in their own time, so we know the names of very few of them. Nevertheless they were devout and humble followers of the Lord, the faithful remnant in Israel. They were the people who recognized Jesus as the Son of God and received him unto their salvation.

These people talked of the things of God in their homes. They prayed to him with deep passion and desire. They hungered and thirsted for righteousness. Their hearts were pure, and their lives made them the leaven of the land.

Anna and Simeon are typical of this vast number. Though advanced in years, their faith was still vibrant. Though rooted in a tradition-rich heritage, they were open to change in their lives. They were prepared to leave the old in order to be part of the Messiah's new age.

While others walked right by the young couple and their child, these two saw him for who he was. They embraced and confessed him. They received the end of their faith, even the salvation of their souls.

The pompous and the irreverent, the professional clergy and the political bigwigs, the disinterested and the pretenders, all passed him by. But the common people heard him gladly. They still do.

THE MAGI

17
MAGI WATCHING THE STARS

What's wrong with the following pictures? Moses on Mt. Sinai typing the Ten Commandments on his notebook computer. Simon Peter calling to shore from his fishing boat for one of his friends to bring him a Pepsi. Mary, Joseph, shepherds, and three men in regal robes bowing before the Holy Baby on the night of his birth.

All three scenes are *anachronistic*. Each puts an object or person out of its proper chronological place. Each misplaces something in relation to the other parts of the event. There were no notebook computers in Moses' time. There were no Pepsis in the Ancient Near East when Peter fished on the Sea of Galilee. And there were no Magi at the original nativity scene.

The mystery surrounding the Wise Men who came to see the Christ-child has spawned a host of legends. The most well-known bit of folklore that passes for history is that there were three Magi and that each was a king. They have even been given names: Caspar, Melchior, and Balthasar. They have been held to represent three major branches of the human race: the Semitic race, other white races, and the black race. At the Cathedral of Cologne, the obituaries of the three are preserved. All three are said to have died in A.D. 55—Caspar at age 109, Melchior at age 116, and Balthasar at age 112. The myths about the men who sought Christ because of a star they saw in the East go on and on.

The notion that there were *three* Wise Men is probably deduced from their offering of three gifts. That they were kings is a tradition traceable as far back as Tertullian, who died around A.D. 225, and may be based on a strained reading of Psalm 72:10-11: "The kings of Tarshish and of distant shores will bring tribute to him; the kings of Sheba and Seba will present him gifts. All kings will bow down to him and all nations will serve him."

The notion that there were three Wise Men is probably deduced from their offering of three gifts.

We actually know next to nothing about the Magi. They came from the East, but that could mean Babylon, Persia, or the Arabian desert. Their identification in the biblical text as Magi (Greek, *magoi*) doesn't tell us a great deal either. The term embraces an assortment of people—ranging from honest seekers of truth to charlatans in search of easy money from gullible people—who studied ancient documents, dreams, and astrology. My assumption is that the ones in Matthew's Gospel were scholars with limited data but unbounded eagerness. They wanted to know God and to do his will.

With regard to the discrepancy of chronology typically reflected in nativity scenes, we can be sure that the Magi did not see baby Jesus in the manger on the night of his birth. For one thing, the text informs us that the little family was living in a "house" by the time the pilgrims from the East arrived at Bethlehem (Matt. 2:11). For another, the expensive gifts they brought would have made it possible for Joseph and Mary to offer a better sacrifice than two birds (the sacrifice of the poorest people who could not afford a lamb) at Mary's purification on the fortieth day following the birth of the child (Luke 2:24). When Herod later calculated backward to the time the Magi had indicated for the appearance of the star they saw, he decided to destroy all the infants two years old and under (Matt. 2:16). Granting that he probably expanded the outer limit a bit so as not to miss the baby in question, this suggests that they saw a several-months-old baby rather than a newborn when they finally arrived at Bethlehem.

From Suetonius and Tacitus, we know that Gentile scholars had somehow learned of the sacred writings of the Jews and knew of their prediction of a Jewish ruler-deliverer. Large Jewish communities in places such as Babylon would account for the spread of this knowledge to men such as the Magi.

Specifically, the thing that moved the Wise Men of our narrative into action was the appearance of a star in the heavens. The star has generated almost as much speculation as the identity of the Magi themselves.

Some suggest it was the explosion of a faint star which gives off a tremendous amount of light for several weeks or a few months, a supernova. Others associate it with an unusual alignment of the planets Jupiter and Saturn that is known to have occurred in 7 B.C. Still others offer an appearance of Halley's Comet in 12 B.C. to explain the heavenly light that called the Magi to the homeland of the Jews. How could such distant phenomena have guided men to the very house where Jesus was?

The more natural explanation of the star—for those who believe at all in the supernatural—is that it was a special sign within Earth's atmosphere that went before the Magi to lead them to the holy child. As the cloud and fire moved before ancient Israel in the wilderness (Exod.13:21), so did a heavenly light move before these travelers from the East. Whether others saw it, we have no way to know. Neither can we be sure that it was before them constantly as the cloud and fire were before the Israelites. "When they saw the star, they were overjoyed" (Matt. 2:10) may mean that a previously visible sign that had brought the men to Palestine reappeared to them after their call on King Herod.

Matthew begins his account of the Magi by informing us that they went to Jerusalem. If the star had originally appeared, been taken as a sign of the appearance of the expected Jewish royal figure, and then disappeared, this route makes perfectly good sense. Where would Easterners be expected to go in search of a Jewish king, if not to Jerusalem? They asked, "Where is the one who has been born king of the Jews? We saw his star in the east and have come to worship him" (Matt. 2:2).

That they were men of some wealth and status is implied from the stir they caused at Jerusalem. Vagabonds passing through and asking about the King of the Jews would get curious looks, perhaps, but not the official notice these men received. When King Herod heard about the city's notable visitors and learned what they were looking for, he was disturbed. More than that, the whole city got upset. And well it might be unsettled.

Everything we know about King Herod is consistent with the things Matthew tells about his involvement in this story. Born somewhere around 73 B.C., Herod was given the title "King of the Jews" in 40 B.C. by the Roman senate. After three years of fighting to establish his rule, he actually reigned over Judea from 37 B.C. until his death in 4 B.C. He was hated by the Jewish populace. They regarded the Idumean Herod as a half-breed usurper propped up in office by the Romans. Though a great builder and politically adept at staying within Roman favor during changes in the Imperial City, the man Herod is a sad study in human depravity.

Always scheming, violent, and unpredictable, he became paranoid in his final years. He was so jealous of his favorite wife (among his ten) that he twice ordered that she be killed if he failed to come back from a dangerous mission. He could not bear to think of another man having Mariamne. He did, in fact, have her put to death before he died. Out of suspicion that some of his sons were plotting to take away his throne, he murdered three of them. It is not surprising that Jerusalem was upset about Herod's discomfiture over a "baby born king of the Jews." It could well become the occasion for a murderous rampage in the city.

Herod did not know the Hebrew Scripture, so he called together the chief priests and teachers of the Law of Moses to get to the bottom of what was happening. They informed him, based on a statement from Micah 5:2, that the Jewish Messiah was to come from Bethlehem of Judah.

An interesting thing about Micah 5:2 is that it is not quoted quite accurately at Matthew 2:6. A closing line from 2 Samuel 5:2 is added to the prophecy so that it reads:

> But you, Bethlehem, in the land of Judah,
>   are by no means least among the rulers
>   of Judah;
> for out of you will come a ruler *who will be the shepherd of my people Israel.*

Whether Matthew or the Jerusalem scholars advising Herod altered the verse to include that line is difficult to say. In either case, the prospect of a ruler who would treat the Jews with a shepherd's concern rather than Herodian contempt is a stark contrast in the text.

With the information he needed in hand, Herod dismissed the Jewish teachers and summoned the visiting Gentile scholars to a private meeting. He wanted to know the "exact time" when the star had appeared to them, and then he started them on their journey. Then he sent them on to Bethlehem with this charge: "Go and make a careful search for the child. As soon as you find him, report to me, so that I too may go and worship him." Worship him? . . . Destroy him! But he had to say that to the Magi so they wouldn't suspect anything. Apparently they didn't at that point and would have returned to give the child's location to Herod except for a dream that later warned them against doing so.

After their audience with King Herod, the Magi were on their way again. The star moved in front of them and finally "stopped over the place where the child was." To some, this means that it identified the very house where the child could be found, as if a helicopter searchlight were shining on a target. Perhaps it means only that the star led them to Bethlehem and stopped. This would indicate that they were in the right city and allow them to inquire after the child in the town where shepherds had earlier spread the word of his birth (Luke 2:17-18).

When they came to the house where Joseph, Mary, and Jesus were, it may have been a sight for which they were unprepared. If the Magi were men of substance and rank, Luther's suggestion that the humble dwelling of a Jewish peasant family was probably a great trial to them is on target. Had they made their long journey to find a king here? It is a testimony to the sincerity of their faith that they entered the house.

137

When they did go inside, they saw the child with his mother. Then, Matthew writes, they "bowed down and worshipped him" (Matt. 2:11). Scholars bowed low before a baby. Literate men paid homage to the child of peasants. Gentiles worshipped a Jew.

What could they have known about the baby at that point? How well informed could their worship have been? Was it more of pagan superstition and noisy gyrations so typical of eastern religion of that time rather than the restrained reverence westerners tend to read into the scene?

How did Joseph and Mary react? Were they embarrassed? Could they have been offended? Was the baby startled? Might he have cried out?

Conscientious seekers of the truth were in the presence of deity. They were there at God's call. Beyond that, they had neither information nor a worship program. So they bowed. They worshipped. They gave what they had—humble, believing, devoted hearts.

Then, having already given themselves, they presented him the gifts they had brought with them. Out of their personal treasure boxes, they presented gold, frankincense, and myrrh. They offered gold, the precious metal that remains a universal medium of exchange. They gave frankincense, a fragrant resin extracted from trees and used as incense at the temple. They delivered myrrh, a very expensive perfume often used in preparing corpses for burial.

How long they stayed is not told. What we do know about their departure is that it was not via Jerusalem and Herod's court. They were warned in a dream not to reveal the baby's whereabouts to King Herod, so they returned to their country by another route. What conversations they must have had along the way!

---

*Literate men paid homage
to the child of peasants.
Gentiles worshipped a Jew.*

"Is that what you expected to find?" one might have asked the others.

"That little house would hardly pass for the residence of a king!" would have been a natural reply.

Did the warning against sharing his whereabouts with Herod make them suspicious of the danger that lay ahead for the child? Did they try to figure out their own future responsibilities in relation to the child? Did they live long enough to know anything of his adult career? Perhaps we can get answers to these questions in heaven, but there is nothing more about the men in Scripture. They leave the scene as suddenly as they entered it. The growth of legends such as the ones mentioned at the beginning of this chapter shows the degree of curiosity that has surrounded them from ancient times until now.

If shepherds watching their flocks near Bethlehem were included in the birth story to signify that God breaks into the routine of people's lives to show his glory and that he accepts the outcasts of society, what justifies the inclusion of the Magi? If Simeon and Anna watching the temple courts shows that it takes a certain sensitivity to recognize God's presence, what is shown by the Magi watching stars?

First, the story of the Magi does not make astrology legitimate. The full array of superstition that goes under the general heading of *occultism* is dealt with severely in the Word of God. Deuteronomy 18:9-14 contains a scathing denunciation of it all, calling such things "detestable practices" that God's people must renounce.

If anything, the astrology of ancient times was more respectable than today's versions. It embraced a variety of educated people who today would be given more respectable titles as astronomers, mathematicians, philosophers, and theologians. Astrology itself, however, has always been nothing higher on the intellectual scale than a superstition. It is a fatalistic view of human destiny that seeks the meaning of human life in the movements of the stars rather than in the will of the God who created the stars.

There is no reason to think that first-century astrologers were any more adept at reading the stars for the true meaning of history than their modern counterparts who offer inane counsel in the daily newspaper. That the Magi of this story were brought to the Christ-child is a testimony to divine grace rather than to astrology. God's decision to save Rahab no more endorses her prostitution or lying than does his gracious call of these men to Bethlehem sanction astrology.

Second, the Magi's presence more likely reflects God's willingness to reveal himself to Gentiles, as well as Jews, through the child born at Bethlehem. The shepherds were surely righteous men of Israel, albeit social outcasts and religiously disenfranchised. Simeon and Anna, on the other hand, were devout people within the ranks of the temple regulars. Both would be embraced by the Son of God. But would there be any place for non-Israelites?

> *It is more important to know a person's attitude toward the truth he discovers than to know his present beliefs.*

Whether they understood their messages or not, Old Testament prophets such as Isaiah were moved by the Spirit of God to predict the sharing of salvation with "all nations" under the Messiah's reign (Isa. 2:1-2). Simeon had praised God for the child who would be "a light for revelation to the Gentiles" (Luke 2:32a). The summoning of the Magi was the initial fulfillment of these promises to people outside the covenant community of Israel.

Third, and most important, the Magi symbolize the hope we have for every truth seeker from whatever culture or background. Do some people search after God in sincerity from different departure points than my own? Or yours? It is typically more important to know a person's attitude toward the truth he discovers than to know his present beliefs.

A gentle and sincere lady in Japan began attending Christian worship at the invitation of a neighbor she had come to respect. As I heard her describe the experience, she told how offended she was by the loud preaching (surely modeled after the American method of sermonizing) and the poor singing. But she continued to attend occasionally over a period of six or seven years. All the while, she continued to worship at the shrines of her traditional religion and to venerate her ancestors. Very slowly her heart began to open to the message of Christ, and she became a Christian late in life.

Her starting point did not make her a likely prospect for the gospel. The method of teaching to which she was exposed was not very effective and may have delayed her salvation. The critical factor was the attitude of her heart to the truth God revealed to her.

Magi from the East, dabblers in astrology, devotees of the New Age Movement, members of far-left or far-right political groups, HIV-infected athletes, campus demonstrators, prisoners, street people—all may seem unlikely candidates for the gospel to you. But there are good and honest hearts everywhere you turn in this world. While the percentage of such hearts might reasonably be higher in some settings than in others, we must be cautious about our judgments. We are to be salt and light wherever we go. God will draw those whom he seeks from whatever unlikely source he chooses.

God does not await our permission to draw people to his Beloved Son. He is doing that constantly. But he does want us to participate in receiving them into his kingdom, lest our coldness to them become the final, insurmountable barrier that keeps them from Christ.

The Magi came. Joseph and Mary welcomed them into the presence of the Son of God. They offered their worship. God accomplished his purposes.

Does God still call men to himself today? Do all come from the backgrounds we would like? Do they offer the same form or intensity of worship we do? So long as we welcome them into the presence of the Son of God by the faithful proclamation of the gospel, is God not able to accomplish his purposes in them?

18

DISTRACTED BY KNOWLEDGE

Knowledge can be a wonderful thing. It also can be a substitute for action, an alternative to obedience, a distraction from God.

When Magi from the East went in search of the baby born King of the Jews, they did a very reasonable thing. They stopped at Jerusalem, the holy city of the Jews. They made inquiries. After all, Jerusalem was the place where the reigning King of the Jews, Herod the Great, lived. Perhaps they thought the child had been born in his palace.

When Herod learned of their presence and questions, he also did a reasonable thing. He called the chief priests and teachers of the Law of Moses to ask what Scripture said about the birth of Israel's long-awaited Messiah. They were able to cite Micah's prophecy concerning Bethlehem and answer his question with authority.

But the behavior of the Jewish priests and leaders was bizarre and unreasonable. They went back to their scrolls and libraries. There is no indication that any of them headed off to Bethlehem with the Magi.

Doesn't that strike you as a bit strange? With all the anxiety in Israel about the Messiah's coming, these scholars in the sacred text were too caught up in their studies to get involved in the event itself. Wanting to know every detail of God in his written word, they seem to have been totally unwilling to take any steps to know God in his person.

These scholars of the sacred text were too caught up in their studies to get involved in the event itself.

Academic types have that sort of reputation. I have had some teachers whose lecture notes were more important to them than their students, whose time for research was so important that their families were shoved aside, whose only life was in books rather than in reality.

The pity is all the greater if the myopic students are biblical scholars whose work gets in the way of their personal knowledge of the Son of God. So a homiletics professor flees to the classroom rather than face "demanding church members" in a local church. A seminary has an expert in the literature of evangelism who is not leading lost people to Christ. A church has a pastor who is known to the flock by his picture in the foyer rather than by his involvement in their lives.

Don, the high school football coach, was a super teacher in the senior high department. It was largely his instruction and influence one winter quarter that led Chris, a high school junior, to confess Jesus and be baptized. Chris' faith suffered a real jolt, though, when the team lost its Homecoming game that fall and he overheard the coach's foul-mouthed berating of his players as they left the field for the locker room.

People whose knowledge of God is cerebral rather than existential are hopeless. Demons know that God exists, but they are demons precisely because their knowledge produced no submission or holiness before him (James 2:18-20).

If the infant Jesus could have spoken a message to the scholars in Herod's court, surely it would have been the same one he gave to some men during his adult ministry: "You diligently study the Scriptures because you think that by them you possess eternal life. These are the Scriptures that testify about me, yet you refuse to come to me to have life" (John 5:39-40).

Writing books about Jesus is no substitute for knowing him as Savior and Lord. Teaching Sunday school classes must not become an alternative to holy living. Reverent reading of the Bible won't replace obeying its Author.

Don't let the covers of your Bible become blinders to keep you from seeing Christ or the people he has called you to love and serve in his name.

THE AUTHORITIES

19
HIDDEN AGENDAS

When an insecure, paranoid, and murderous Herod the Great heard of a child who had been born to be King of the Jews, he pretended to have a reverent interest in the event. He learned what he could from the biblical scholars retained at his court. That wasn't very much, however, for they could only cite the prophecy of Micah that the Lord's Messiah would be born in Bethlehem.

When Herod passed that information on to the Magi searching for the baby, he linked the disclosure with a request. "Go and make a careful search for the child," he told them. "As soon as you find him, report to me, so that I too may go and worship him."

Ha! Worship the child indeed! He wanted to sever his head. He would have no misgiving about running him through with a sword. Neither would he lose sleep over tossing him to wild animals or burning him to ashes.

How dare Herod use so sacred a sentiment as *worship* to mask his murderous scheme!

Before we voice too much indignation and feel too self-assured, though, it would be wise to take stock of our own hearts. Human motivation is often mixed. A shady purpose is shrouded beneath noble rhetoric. A corrupt plan is concealed behind a holy pretense.

Herod was neither the first person—nor the last—to operate with a *hidden agenda*. In the name of having a good time, thousands of kids have lied to their parents about going to a movie, then spaced themselves out with drugs or alcohol, and put themselves into hospitals . . . or morgues. In the name of love, many a woman has been manipulated to eschew virginity, commitment, and virtue, only to be left to weep alone, feeling used and soiled.

> *A corrupt plan is often concealed behind a holy pretense.*

In the name of religion, people have built personal empires and taken the life savings of sincere but duped followers. Sex, sleaze, and scandal replaced faith, hope, and love in their "ministries."

In the name of patriotism, petty politicians have lined their pockets by betraying the public trust. In the name of discipline, parents have been known to beat, burn, break bones, or otherwise abuse defenseless children. In the name of personal freedom, all of us have now and then declared our independence of God, Scripture, or law to go our own self-willed ways.

Jeremiah once lamented that the human heart is "deceitful above all things." I can only wonder how many Herod-type personalities he had met to that point in his life. How many you have met to this point in yours?

20

WHO IS REALLY KING?

*P*ower. It is an important word in the human vocabulary. It can mean vastly different things.

On the one hand, power can be understood as the right to command, order, manipulate, and control others. This is what we mean by the word when we use it in most political, business, and social settings. The person with power is the one who is at the top of the pyramid. He calls the shots. She throws her weight around. He bosses and cajoles until he gets his way. She consolidates power until the time comes to make her move.

Some villainous characters have left their marks in history via the exercise of this sort of power. Thus we remember names like Nebuchadnezzar, Ghengis Khan, Adolf Hitler, and Idi Amin. Satan offered this kind of power to Jesus when he showed him "all the kingdoms of the world and their splendor" and said, "All this will I give you, if you will bow down and worship me" (Matt. 4:8-9).

On the other hand, though, there is a form of power that does not depend on titles, armies, or money. It is the power a child has over her father. It is the power of a lover with his beloved. Or it is Barnabas' exercise of power with a rejected Saul and a crushed John Mark.

People with power of this second variety most often step aside for rather than step ahead of others. They don't threaten or manipulate; they liberate and empower. They refuse to use the lies or bribes that seem to go hand in hand with power of the sort described earlier. They deal in truth, candor, and honest challenge.

No one has ever used power this healthy way so perfectly as Jesus of Nazareth. He never manipulated or took advantage of anyone. He didn't swagger and boast. He didn't intimidate with titles or dress, pomp or exhibition.

He loved children. He showed compassion to an immoral Samaritan woman and dealt gently with the publican Zacchaeus, without patronizing either. He demonstrated patience with thick-headed disciples who were aghast that he would perform so menial a task as washing feet and who kept pressing him to establish a kingdom on the traditional model of political power—with themselves, of course, filling key posts of distinction.

In connection with his entry into flesh, Jesus precipitated the first of many clashes centered on the power issue. It makes an interesting case study.

Jesus was born during the time and under the territorial rule of King Herod. Most often called Herod the Great, the Romans allowed him to be their puppet king in Judea. In the year 40 B.C., the Roman senate gave him the title "King of the Jews."

Herod's father was an Idumean Jew named Antipater. Idumea was located in the area just south of Judea, and, at the point of a sword, its inhabitants had accepted the religion of the Jews only two generations before Herod's birth. Herod's mother was an Arab princess.

There is a form of power that does not depend on titles, armies, or money.

Because he had assisted Octavian in his campaigns in neighboring Egypt, Antipater was made the Roman procurator of Palestine in 55 B.C. Until his assassination in 43 B.C., he played shrewd politics with the Romans and maintained power.

After Antipater's death, the Romans needed a loyal ally in the Jewish territory who would protect their interests against the intentions of a priestly group wanting to throw off all foreign presence and power. It was in this context that Herod was given the title King of the Jews. But was he *really* their king?

When the Romans declared him king, Antigonus, a member of the priestly Hasmonean group, was in control of Jerusalem and had taken the title of king to himself. With Rome's aid, Herod fought for three years

to gain control of the region. He had Antigonus crucified and beheaded. Herod also decreed the execution
of over forty priests who had opposed his ascension to
power.

Just before he captured Jerusalem and began his
actual rule over the Jews in 37 B.C., he married a
Jewish woman of the Hasmonean line named
Mariamne. By means of this marriage, he hoped to
mitigate the widespread hatred of the people toward
him as a non-Jew. Strangely enough, the evidence
seems to suggest that he came to love Mariamne more
than any other of his ten wives.

A suspicious man, King Herod always saw people
scheming against him. Considering the Hasmoneans
to be primary enemies, he set about to eliminate them
one by one. Eventually he put even Mariamne to death
for plotting against him in 29 B.C. He had his two sons
by her, Alexander and Aristobulus, who were brought
up in Rome and designated as his heirs in Judea. But
they were also judged guilty of conspiring against their
father and executed in 7 B.C.

For all his personal and political wickedness,
Herod was a genius as a professional builder. He built
the spectacular mountain citadel at Masada on the
Dead Sea. In an attempt to win the loyalty of the
Jewish people who despised him as a man of mixed
blood, he began a lavish reconstruction project of the
Second Jewish Temple at Jerusalem in 19 B.C. The
project was not completed until A.D. 63, nearly seventy
years after his death.

Fear built Masada, and the temple at Jerusalem
was a failed attempt at buying a nation's loyalty. But

the Roman garrison town of Caesarea was Herod's most colossal work of self-expression. It was built as a monument that would consolidate his power, enrich his coffers, and certify his fame.

Herod built the city in the twelve years between 22 and 10 B.C. He named it for his patron, Caesar Augustus, the first Roman Emperor. An aqueduct that required tunneling through four miles of solid rock brought water from Mount Carmel to its Roman baths and fountains. He built a large harbor in the open sea without any protective bay or peninsula. Using a concrete mixture that hardened when it came into contact with water, his engineers surpassed anything the Romans had ever done with the concrete construction technique they had invented two centuries earlier. At least one hundred ships of the time could anchor in its protected waters.

So as to pursue and fund his passion for building, Herod had to play the power game with consummate skill. He had to placate his overlords in Rome and preserve his base of jurisdiction among the Jews of his Judean kingdom. He was never very subtle about preserving his mastery. He was ruthless and cold-blooded in dealing with anyone who represented a threat to his position.

Even Emperor Caesar Augustus commented caustically, "I would rather be Herod's pig than his son." In Greek, there is a mocking play on words in Augustus' remark. *Huios* is the word for son, while *hus* is the word for pig.

In Herod's death agony, he ordered the arrest of a group of Jerusalem elite. At his death, they were to be executed so that tears would be shed on the day he died. When he died the order was countermanded as that of a madman, so it is unlikely that any tears fell for Herod the Great when he expired in 4 B.C. In the words of one historian, "He stole to the throne like a fox, ruled like a tiger, and died like a dog."

What we know of this King of the Jews as a figure of history fits perfectly with what we know of his behavior toward the birth of a child destined to be "King of the Jews." What a jolt it must have been for nervous, jealous Herod when visitors from the East came to his court and asked about a baby destined to rule over the Jews. As Matthew relates, "After Jesus was born in Bethlehem in Judea, during the time of King Herod, Magi from the east came to Jerusalem and asked, 'Where is the one who has been born king of the Jews? We saw his star in the east and have come to worship him'" (Matt. 2:1-2).

The wise men made a tragic mistake, but it was an understandable one. If one were looking for the birthplace of the new Jewish king, where better to inquire than at the palace of the reigning king? What these strangers knew about Herod and his paranoia is unknown. More than likely, they knew practically nothing about him except that he was King of the Jews. The machinations of such a petty monarch would not have been a topic of interest in Persia, Babylon, or any other eastern country. Let's not fault the Magi, then, for a blunder we see in hindsight but which they could not have foreseen.

In a classic instance of understatement, Matthew writes, "When King Herod heard this he was disturbed" (Matt. 2:3a). Disturbed? He must have been unsettled to the depths of his soul! And he must have turned in a masterful performance before his guests to restrain his anger. Can't you imagine, however, that all eyes darted around the room when the question was put to him: "Where is the one who has been born King of the Jews?" His court knew that Herod had killed his own wives and children when he thought they threatened his reign as Jewish monarch.

The understatement continues when Matthew says that "all Jerusalem [was disturbed] with him" (Matt. 2:3b). They knew the unpredictable rage of this power-mad Idumean. It was not beyond anyone's imagination in Jerusalem that Herod would set about to search houses and kill children. In fact, the locals must have been surprised at the restrained response to his visitors.

King Herod called together the chief priests and teachers of the Law of Moses. He asked for whatever light they could shed on the matter. Had they heard of a star? Were there rumors about a baby? Did their Scripture have anything to say on the matter?

As a matter of fact, they responded, their holy books contained a prediction about the Messiah's birth. Thus they told Herod that he was to be born in Bethlehem and cited the prophecy on which they based their belief: "But you, Bethlehem, in the land of Judah, are by no means least among the rulers of Judah; for out of you will come a ruler who will be the shepherd of my people Israel" (Matt. 2:6; cf. Mic. 5:2).

Furnished with this information, King Herod called the Magi for a final, private interview. Before telling them what he had learned, he first pressed them for additional details about their experience. What sort of "star" did you see? How did you know that you were supposed to follow it? Exactly when did you first see it?

Then, after learning all he could from them, he passed on the information about Bethlehem. From the way Matthew describes the scene, Herod appears to have tried hard to avoid raising any suspicions among his guests. He simply sent them to Bethlehem, five or six miles from Jerusalem, and told them to "make a careful search" for the newborn king. "As soon as you find him," he instructed the Magi, "report to me, so that I too may go and worship him" (Matt. 2:7).

Apparently still naive about King Herod and the plans he might have for the baby they were searching for, the eastern stargazers left for Bethlehem. They must have left the king's court with a sense of confirmation about their mission and with renewed excitement. The heavenly sign they had been following led them not just to the town of Bethlehem but to the very house in which the baby and his family were living.

They entered, worshipped the child, and presented the gifts they had brought to him. Did they stay in Jerudalem for just the one visit? Were they in Bethlehem for several days? The text of the Bible leaves us without a clue. What we are told about their departure returns the focus to Herod the Great: "And having been warned in a dream not to go back to Herod, they returned to their country by another route" (Matt. 2:12).

How long did Herod wait for word from the Magi? Probably not very long. Nervous and insecure as he was, he would soon have concluded that someone had gotten wise to him and that his guests were not coming back with word of the child. The man whose fear of rivals had already bathed his own family in blood dispatched soldiers to dispose of this latest one.

Calculating back to the time when the Magi had first seen the star, perhaps allowing another six to twelve months for good measure, King Herod gave orders that all the boys in Bethlehem and its vicinity who were two years old and under were to be killed. Given the size of Bethlehem at the time as a town of 1,500 to 2,000 people and an annual birthrate of perhaps thirty children per thousand, the number of male infants murdered by Herod would likely have been no less than twelve and no more than twenty-four. There is no non-biblical record of the event. Given the obscurity of the town and the grosser cruelties of Herod, we are not surprised that this atrocity doesn't survive in ancient archives.

In the meanwhile, Jesus was miraculously saved from death. Joseph was warned in a dream about Herod's plot and fled Bethlehem in the middle of the night to save Jesus (Matt. 2:13-15). What awkward-sounding language! Jesus, the Savior of the World, was saved by faithful Joseph.

Herod wielded his power as King of the Jews. He built his towers, fortifications, and cities. He fought armies and murdered babies. Then, two or three years after Jesus was born in Bethlehem, King Herod died, unmourned.

What has been the verdict of history on these two figures? King Herod is a footnote to history; King

Jesus is the one from whose coming all history is dated.

Years ago, someone summed up the impact of Jesus with these words:

> Here is a young man who was born in an obscure village, the child of a peasant woman. He grew up in another village. He worked in a carpenter's shop until he was grown, and then for three years he was an itinerant preacher.
>
> He never wrote a book. He never held an office. He never owned a home. He never had a family. He never went to college. He never put his foot inside a really big city. He never traveled over 200 miles from the place where he was born. He never did any of the things that usually accompany greatness. He had no credentials but himself.
>
> While he was still a young man, the tide of public opinion turned against him. His friends ran away. He was turned over to his enemies. He went through the mockery of a trial. He was nailed to a cross between two thieves. While he was dying, his executioners gambled for the only piece of property he had on earth—his coat. When he was dead, he was laid in a borrowed grave through the pity of a friend.
>
> Nineteen centuries have come and gone, and today he is the central figure of the human race and the leader of the column of progress.
>
> I am well within the mark when I say that all the armies that ever marched, all the navies that ever sailed, all the parliaments that ever sat, and all the kings that ever reigned—put together—have not affected the life of man upon this earth as has that one solitary life.

So who is *really* king? Is it the one who bullies, pushes, and destroys with his power? Or is it the one who loves, serves, and empowers others?

The kingdoms of this world and all whose hearts are dominated by the sinful nature can only model the Herodian ideal. The Kingdom of God and the hearts of those who are indwelt by the Spirit of God must put on the new garments of compassion, forgiveness, and love. Where these traits are lived, the Babe of Bethlehem reigns. He is Sovereign, Lord of Lords, and King of Kings.

THE CHILD

21

IMMANUEL

It certainly isn't the most common name in the world: *Immanuel.*

I wonder if anyone other than Joseph and Mary ever used it of him? My dad used to call me to the front of his store or in from play with a name no one else ever used for me. "Joe, would you come here a minute?" I knew whom he was calling, but hardly anyone else did. Do you suppose Joseph called Jesus to his workbench or inside from playing with a name others in Nazareth never used of him? "Immanuel, would you come here a minute?"

Can you imagine what that name signified to Mary and Joseph? Sure, lots of names have meanings that parents hope will attach to their children. Timothy means "God-fearer." Dorothy means "gift of God." Ethan means "strong." Katherine means "pure." The name Immanuel means "God with us."

When Joseph or Mary used that name of the little boy in their house, they must have felt awestruck. They knew the real paternity of their son, and they accepted his presence with them as the Son of God. He was divine, their Sovereign Lord, the Creator. God was with them in a unique way.

Imagine them staring at him and thinking about his identity. Then imagine the baby sneezing, burping, or wetting his diaper. He was a real baby, you know! What would they think then? Jesus is the world's greatest and most startling paradox.

> *They knew the real paternity of their son, and they accepted his presence with them as the Son of God.*

Maybe they never used Immanuel as a proper name at all. Perhaps it was simply a descriptive term like mountain climber, musician, or mother-in-law. When we use those terms, we are not naming people. We are describing a distinctive or notable feature of their functions in life. If that is how we are to understand Immanuel, things other than parental endearment or paradox come to mind.

Immanuel means that heaven is no longer remote from Earth. *God with us* signifies that we have worth in his eyes, that he cares what goes on among us, that he loves us. Immanuel means that we have seen God with skin on and know how we should think and behave and treat one another if we want to be godly people.

God with us defines the meaning of goodness, mercy, faithfulness, and love. Immanuel means that we are not isolated from a God on a distant throne, but that we have a God who is able to sympathize with our weaknesses.

At a more personal level, however, perhaps his name or title needs to be pronounced "God with *us*" rather than "*God* with us" or "God *with* us." The real point of Jesus in my life is not that he was born at Bethlehem, reared at Nazareth, or crucified at Jerusalem. The truth of those things means nothing until he is in me and I in him.

Immanuel must be translated "God with *me*" in order to mean salvation. And when that presence is real, it is as impossible to miss as a curious child with quick hands in a carpenter's shop or his dozens of questions at his mother's knee.

A latter-day Mary, who was far removed from either virginity or holiness, fell under the weight of her sin. She made a serious attempt to kill herself, only to be snatched back to life after a roommate came home early and called the paramedics. Mary was anything but grateful.

Now, four-and-one-half years later, Mary has her act together. She is sane and responsible. She is a productive human being. She is at church every time the doors are open. At her job, she is serving Christ by working with disabled children. And she has been married for nearly a year to a Christian man who loves her devotedly.

What happened to Mary, you ask? She decided to let God be with her. She is living the truth of *Immanuel.*

Mary had known about him from childhood. The struggles of painful teen years took her far away from him. Finally, with her empty life handed back to her after the suicide attempt, she looked back in his direction. She stopped fighting God. She believed. She surrendered. She adopted the attitude of her biblical namesake: "I am the Lord's servant. May it be to me as you have said."

It still happens—wherever a noncoercive God is received into a humble and teachable heart.

> *Immanuel.*
> *Hallelujah!*
> *Maranatha!*

22
THAT'S INCREDIBLE!

Remember the television show of a few years back called "That's Incredible"? It featured snake charmers, people who walked on live coals, unusual buildings, bizarre pets, and daredevils leaping cars on motorcycles.

But here is the single most incredible event that has happened in all human history:

> The Word became flesh and made his dwelling
> among us.
> —*John*

> [Christ Jesus], being in very nature God,
> did not consider equality with God something
> to be grasped,
> but made himself nothing,
> taking the very nature of a servant,
> being made in human likeness.
> — *Paul*

> All praise to Thee, Eternal Lord,
> Clothed in a garb of flesh and blood;
> Choosing a manger for a throne,
> While worlds are Thine alone.
> —*Martin Luther*

The notion of incarnation is genuinely incredible. Extraordinary, startling, fantastic—a host of adjectives could be used to describe it.

Someone who is so bound up in this world that he cannot admit the idea of a divine being who could enter his own creation finds other words to describe it. Absurd, impossible, insane, this list of adjectives can also go on ad infinitum.

Porphyry was a third-century scholar who is remembered in textbooks as one of the founders of Neoplatonism. He was emphatic in his reaction to the idea of incarnation. "How can one admit that the divine should become an embryo," he asked in his vicious *Against the Christians,* "that after his birth he is put in swaddling clothes, that he is soiled with blood and bile, and worse things yet?"

Why would a divine being leave the perfection of his ideal environment to come to Earth?

The cardinal objection to the idea seems to be a very natural one. Why would a divine being leave the perfection of his ideal environment to come to Earth? So Arnobius, in his *Adversus nationes,* wrote, "If souls were of the Lord's race, they would permanently dwell in the king's court, without ever leaving that place of beatitude. . . . They would never come to these terrestrial places where they inhabit opaque bodies and are mixed with humors and blood, in receptacles of excrement, in vases of urine."

Think about it! Have you had any serious thoughts lately about moving from your two-bedroom house or apartment into a crowded slum? Are you considering giving up your home for a bedroll to go live among the homeless? What would you say about leaving the comfort of your home to join a leper colony in India and empty the bedpans of its sickest patients? I don't know what to offer as a comparison to what he did. In all honesty, however, I cannot say that I am shocked at the reaction of horror that serious thinkers have to the incarnation.

The only reason I can offer for the Eternal Word's incredible exploit of coming and living as one of us is unsuited for philosophic argument. Against Porphyry and Arnobius, it likely counts for nothing.

> Why did my Savior come to earth,
> And to the humble go?
> Why did he choose a lowly birth?
> Because he loves me so!

Once in the history of the world, someone came among the human race and dared to claim "Whoever has seen me has seen God" and "I am in the Father and the Father is in me." The proof of his claim was not lofty arguments about esoteric topics in metaphysics but humble identification with the poorest and guiltiest of the race. The presentation of his person was not with pageantry and a retinue of servants, but he took our miseries to himself and washed our feet.

Perhaps Porphyry and Arnobius and a host of other unbelievers insist still that they could only be impressed with a God who shows himself dramatically and powerfully. They would have to be impressed with overwhelming logic and irresistible personal presence. They demand to see him in regal elegance and at a deferential distance from his creatures. Yet Jesus comes and reveals a God who cares about *me*, shares my frailty, and has compassion for my fallenness.

Precisely because of his great love for us, Jesus refused to stagger our minds with philosophers' arguments. Instead, he offered himself in a manger. Instead of a syllogism, he presented light to a dark world. In the place of astonishing logic, he spoke the elegant language of amazing grace.

The incarnation affirms a God who descends to the depths in order to bring his fallen creatures to glory. Now *that* is truly incredible.

23
BABY, DO YOU KNOW . . . ?

Baby in a manger, do you know how far you traveled to be here tonight? Do you remember what you left behind?

Do you realize that you created the world you are visiting? Do you know you made the universe you passed through to get here?

Can you possibly have any idea tonight of the price you will pay for coming to Earth?

Tiny babe, do you know that there have been rumors about your mother because of your birth? Is your sleep disturbed tonight by the knowledge that those rumors will haunt you throughout your stay among men?

Do you know what agony Joseph went through before he decided to claim you and to let you be known as "the carpenter's son"?

Baby, can you tell me the identity of your real Father? Can you say his name?

Do you know that your six-month-old cousin John will become a preacher, too? Are you aware that you will someday ask him to baptize you? Do you realize that he will die by having his head cut off?

Do you know that shepherds who live nearby are on their way to see you tonight? Do you chuckle that angels you knew in heaven sent them to find you?

Baby, are you aware that Magi from a great distance are already traveling this way in search of you?

Can you possibly have any idea tonight of the price you will pay for coming to Earth?

Do you know what gifts they will present you when they arrive a few months from now?

Do you know already who will love you before they have even heard of you or seen you?

Holy child, do you recognize any of these names: Anna? Peter? Herodias? James? Pilate?

Do these places make you think of anything tonight: Egypt? Bethany? Jacob's well? Golgotha?

Do you realize what is at stake for the entire human race with regard to your birth? Is it in your mind that your coming signals the moment of decision for every one of us?

Do you know where Jerusalem is? Can you possibly have any idea what awaits you in that city? Do you want to go there? Are you anxious to get it over and go back home?

Do you know me? Are you aware that I love you? Do you know tonight that you have been born to be my Savior? Does it register for you now that my life will be directed at every critical juncture by halting and imperfect attempts to do your will? Do you know that we will be together in heaven forever?

Baby in Bethlehem, newborn from Mary's womb tonight, do you know who you are?

THEN AND NOW

24

THINGS HAVEN'T CHANGED MUCH

It's hard to say what bothers me most about the situation back then.

Was it all the gossip at Nazareth about Mary and Joseph? Was it Bethlehem's apparent insensitivity to a man and his pregnant wife? Was it Herod's murderous plot to kill the baby? All these disturb me greatly, but something else looms larger than any of them.

For every gossip at Nazareth, there were probably two dozen who cared nothing that one more girl in the town was pregnant before she was married. They were so used to it that nothing shocked them anymore. So what?

Were Bethlehem's innkeepers rude to Joseph? Maybe that tradition is all wrong. Perhaps they were polite in their "no vacancy" speeches. The result, however, was the same. Poor people were left to fend for themselves on a night when they needed reassurance of God's presence.

Was Herod guilty of infanticide? Without a doubt! For the sake of protecting himself and his position, helpless human life was deemed worthless and expendable. And a host of nameless somebodies carried out his execution orders and became murderers in the process.

Today there are still more people who cluck their tongues, pass along the report, and feel self-righteous over skyrocketing teenage pregnancy rates than there are people helping those frightened little girls to find direction for their lives.

We haven't learned nearly as much from Christ's coming as we should have.

Every city of any size has homeless people who are in their plight for reasons as legitimate as Joseph's and Mary's that night in Bethlehem. You've never spit on one of them, have you? You've never called one a "worthless, no-good bum." In these civilized times of ours, we have learned to be ever so polite in telling street people who call our churches that we have no way to help them. Meanwhile, people continue to sleep under bridges, in cardboard lean-tos, and with animals.

And Herod was a small-time operator compared to the elimination of unwanted babies that goes on today. Now it is legally sanctioned and socially acceptable.

Abortions are performed by the thousands every day across the United States.

Two thousand years ago, the world at large took no notice at all of what was going on in it. People just didn't care about any of the issues or the people involved.

Perhaps my problem with both then and now has taken definition. *Things now are too much as they were then.* We haven't learned nearly as much from Christ's coming as we should have, even on the most obvious of things. We don't notice. We don't care enough. We don't change things.

Maybe it's too late. But I hope not.

25

How Chance Serves God's Purpose

Some who read these lines are living shattered lives caused by bankruptcy, illness, pain, job loss, or death of a spouse. The causes of human heartache are too extensive to list.

Many of those same readers will wonder what their situation means in terms of the will of God. Did God will you to lose your house, get cancer, be unemployed, or be a widower? Did he do it to get your attention? Was he trying to teach you a lesson? Somebody has probably offered you one or more of these interpretations of your predicament.

The view that suffering is always God's will or a message from him is naive at best and tends to weaken faith. This was the opinion Job's friends voiced about his awful plight. It was the theory Jesus' disciples advanced about a man who was blind from birth. It was wrong then, and it is wrong now.

The options for interpreting life are sometimes reduced to these two: (1) unbelief holds that what happens, happens, and (2) faith sees all things happening because God wills them so. A third possibility seems to escape the purview of someone who sees things so simplistically. Why can we not grant that many—or, more likely, most—things that happen in our experience are non-purposive, random, and indiscriminate, but that God's will can be achieved in all things through our faith in and obedience to him?

This third alternative permits us to make sense of disparate biblical statements. On the one hand we read: "God causes his sun to rise on the evil and the good" (Matt. 5:45) and "God does not show favoritism" (Acts 10:34). On the other we hear "When [God] has tested me I will come forth as gold" (Job 23:10) and "God disciplines us for our good, that we may share in his holiness" (Heb. 12:10).

A chance incident in connection with the birth of Jesus both illustrates and enlightens this point.

As Joseph and Mary were anticipating the soon-to-be-born Immanuel, "Caesar Augustus issued a decree that a census should be taken of the entire Roman world" (Luke 2:1). Augustus was the first emperor of Rome and ruled from 30 B.C. to A.D. 14. He worked hard to centralize the empire for the sake of its administration, and one of his means to that end was census taking. It was a headcount throughout the provinces that entered a person's name, place of residence, and assets in the public registers. Its ultimate goal was, of course, to exact tax payments from all the people.

The initial census taken among the Jews would have been concluded around 7 B.C. In connection with this event, Jesus was born in Bethlehem rather than in Nazareth.

Joseph and Mary were from Nazareth in Galilee. They had lived there both before and after their marriage. From what we can tell, they had no plans to live anywhere else. If they were aware of the prophecy of the Messiah's birth at Bethlehem (Mic. 5:2), they were apparently doing nothing to see to it that the child in Mary's womb would be born in David's city.

Since it was very near the time for the baby to be born, it must have been a considerable burden for them to hear the news that they had to go to Joseph's ancestral home for a census. In fact, Mary was not obligated to go. Only the head of the house had to appear and be entered on the census roll. But how could he leave her? He loved her, and he must have considered the possibilities of how people at Nazareth would treat his bride when the time came for the child to be born.

Their neighbors had not blessed their marriage with celebrations. It was clear that they had distanced themselves from this once-respected pair. Now they believed Mary and Joseph had rushed their marriage to cover an illegitimate pregnancy. Might they harm her or the baby? Joseph could not take the chance, so he made travel plans for both himself and his wife. What might they have thought as they got ready to travel?

"I don't understand," Mary might have said to herself. "I agreed to be God's servant to bear this child. Why are things coming unraveled now? What sort of 'sign' is this? Is it of God or of Satan? Why should we be taken away from our families now? Will we be able to get to Bethlehem and back before my baby comes?"

"Why is this happening *now?*" Joseph could have mused. "I have tried to make Mary comfortable here. What will become of us on this journey? What if the baby is born on the way? What if there is no midwife and Mary has problems with her delivery? God, I can't make sense of this. Is there some plan?"

Whether this was plan or happenstance may depend on how you understand predictive prophecies in Scripture. Did God foretell something and then make it happen? Or did he tell in advance what his omniscience saw was coming? It is a critical question. If the former, God tells a thing, forces it to happen, and overrides human freedom. If the latter, God tells only such things as his unique perspective on human life sees us choosing freely.

> *It is a monumental leap from God's purpose being served in a debacle to crediting him with creating it.*

Kathryn was fourteen when she had her first abortion. She had had three before she turned sixteen. The heavy guilt she felt after the abortions led her to alcohol, drugs, jail, and suicide. On the day after her death and before her funeral, her younger sister, Kristen, went to the home of a friend who is a Christian. "Please help me!" she begged. "I don't want my life to be like Kathryn's!"

Her friend shared the good news of Jesus with her. Then, just like the conversion stories in Acts, Kristen confessed Christ and was baptized in his name. That was three years ago. Kristen will graduate from high school next spring and is one of the most responsible and respected teens in her youth group at church.

The other day, somebody said, "I hate that God had to take her sister so as to bring Kristen to her senses. But if that's what it took . . . And who are we to question the ways of God?"

AIDS brings someone to repentance and reconciliation with his family. A job transfer puts a family in new surroundings and seems to save it from death by disinterest. The brain tumor of an eighteen-month-old baby draws his separated parents back into the same house and back into each other's hearts. Poverty sends a man to a church to ask for food, and he finds both groceries and salvation.

It happens over and over again that good endings come from the most unpromising beginnings. God's purpose is served in a situation that looked to be a total disaster to everyone who knew about it.

Be careful, though. It is a monumental leap from God's purpose being served in a debacle to crediting him with creating it. Do people really believe that God puts babies to death in order to teach something to their parents? Do they honestly think he causes car accidents or brain tumors trying to bring people to repentance? To say that what happened to Kathryn was the will of God for the sake of bringing her sister to Christ seems absurd to me. If humans exploited and manipulated people in such bizarre ways, they would be called evil. Shall we credit God with the same things and expect people to praise him for his goodness?

God does not compel (or terrorize) us against our wills. He does not force history to overrule human freedom. Instead, he works within the context of history to achieve his ends. Within the random freedom of happenstance and the moral freedom of women and men made in his image, he works through his surrendered servants to bless them and preserve righteousness.

In such a context, there is a great deal of randomness with health and illness, wealth and poverty, prosperity and adversity. But there is no divine injustice. The same rules of cause and effect apply to all of us. Sunshine and rain are distributed without respect of persons.

The primary benefit to the believer is not that she is exempt from the negatives but that she is not left to herself when they come. She has the comfort of her faith. She has the fellowship of her brothers and sisters. She has prayer to ask—but not demand—intervention from God.

Joseph and Mary fulfilled an Old Testament prediction. It seems doubtful that they realized it at the time. Certainly they had no hand in arranging the circumstance that caused it. They did what they had to do in their little corner of the world and committed themselves to God. He brought about his purpose.

Kristen is a Christian today. A tragic sequence of events brought it about. The horrible fate of her older sister frightened her, humbled her, and opened her heart to God. God brought about his purpose to save Kristen.

I don't believe God made Caesar Augustus call a census at just that moment. And I certainly don't believe in a God who destroys a girl to save her sister. I do believe, however, in a God who acts with such power in history that he is able to bring any circumstance to a right end for the sake of his children and his righteousness.

God reigns—when people acknowledge it and when they don't. God acts, whether through you or me, but never against our wills or without our acquiescence.

It is not true that everything happens for a purpose.

If things are happening in your life today that you cannot understand, don't be surprised. If you can't discern God's purpose for this or that, don't despair. What is happening may not be of God and may not have a designated purpose within his scheme of things. It may be, like Job's trials, rooted in Satan's attempt to overthrow your faith. Perhaps, like the man's blindness, it is an unfortunate and inscrutable mystery of unknowable origin.

It is not true that everything happens for a purpose. But it is true that God's purpose can unfold in whatever happens. His purpose is to save you, to discipline you, to teach you to trust him. He wants to make your heart open to him and tender to your fellow man. It is his intent to let you make a difference in your world and to lead other souls to heaven.

History is the arena of God's glory. As random events unfold and as evil struggles against him, God will continue to achieve his purpose in the lives of Josephs and Marys. These are the people of every generation who experience the unexplainable, believe the inexpressible, obey the invisible. In the lives of such people, God will accomplish his purposes. He will fulfill his promises.

If your life is plagued by confusion today, don't see the confusion as God's will. It isn't. God's will is that you, even in your uncertainty, trust him, do what is right, and leave the ultimate outcome to him. What has happened to you may be neither good nor of God, but your good God has power sufficient to bring you through it to a noble end. Why, that is the promise of Scripture: "And we know that in all things God works for the good of those who love him, who have been called according to his purpose" (Rom. 8:28).

When Joseph came home with word of the census and explained the trip that was involved, I wonder if Mary cried? Did they both cry?

As they made the journey, do you think they knew what lay ahead? Might they have feared running into thieves along the road? Is it possible that they felt forsaken when the only shelter they could find in Bethlehem was a stable? Were they frightened when Mary went into labor?

So many things just don't seem to fit with the storybook image we perpetuate about Joseph and Mary. Isn't it better to see them as real people? They were people like us who had to deal with daily realities without understanding the ultimate significance.

If you are perplexed, discouraged, or frightened today, maybe it will help you to look at life from a perspective between two false extremes. Don't assign your circumstance today to God's manipulation. Simply trust him to be faithful to his promise to get you through it.

26

IF JESUS WERE
BORN TODAY

When God was born into our midst
two thousand years ago, he went to extraordinary
lengths to identify himself with the things we try to
avoid. He came among us in poverty, unsanitary con-
ditions, obscurity, and danger.

Because that event is so far away in time, it has an
air of unreality about it for some of us. One of the
greatest needs each of us has relative to Christ's birth
is to see the real humanity of his situation.

What if the Son of God had not been born in
Roman-dominated Palestine of the first century? What
if he had been born in the WASP-dominated United
States of America on the brink of the twenty-first century? To what lengths might he have gone to identify
with human need? The Old Testament prophecies
would have been cited, and the reality of his arrival
would have been just as unlikely among us as it was
then.

Perhaps he would have been born to a teenage
black girl rather than to a teenage Jewish peasant. He
almost surely wouldn't be born to middle-class whites.

Perhaps his place of birth would have been an overcrowded housing project rather than crowded Bethlehem. I can't imagine that he would be born in a hospital and carried home to the suburbs.

Perhaps his place of birth would have been an overcrowded housing project rather than crowded Bethlehem.

Perhaps the man and woman caring for him at his birth would have been married by a justice of the peace rather than by cutting short a Jewish betrothal. People might have whispered about the date being moved up and called it a shotgun wedding.

Perhaps the announcement of his birth would have been made to migrant farm workers or street people rather than to shepherds watching their flocks. I can't see the story being put on the ABC evening news.

If God went to such lengths then to identify with the dispossessed and powerless, shouldn't we bring their modern-day counterparts into the purview of our compassion? Shouldn't we identify with them rather than avoid them?

Think about it this Christmas.

TRADITIONS OF THE SEASON

27
GIFTS ON A TREE

As with the Christmas holiday itself, the origin of the Christmas tree is not clear in all its details. Scandinavian people once worshipped trees, and one theory is that their conversion to Christianity led them to make evergreens part of their festivals. Maybe so. Maybe not.

Many people think Martin Luther was the first person to put lights on a Christmas tree. On this account, Luther put candles on his tree to portray the beauty of the stars above Bethlehem on the night of Christ's birth. Christmas candles and lights represent Jesus Christ as the Light of the World.

Most of us still put lights on our Christmas trees, though we use UL-approved and safe electric ones instead of Luther's dangerous candles! One little elementary school boy came up to his teacher right after Thanksgiving and asked if he could have some sheets of construction paper. She asked why he needed them, and he said, "We can't afford lights for our Christmas tree this year, and I want to make some out of construction paper." The little boy got his construction paper. And, since his teacher had just bought a set of lights for her tree and had them in her car, he got a set of lights that afternoon, too!

Topping the tree with either a star to represent the one who led the Magi or an angel to represent the angel who appeared to the shepherds is a well-known custom. Then there is the old custom of hanging stars and angels, gilded nuts and cookies, candy canes and strings of cranberries on the tree. In fact, it used to be customary to hang the toys and gifts on the tree.

In Galatians 3, Paul makes an argument about Christ that is clearly rabbinic rather than literary-historical in character. He took the idea of what a tree could symbolize under certain circumstances and explained a profound truth about the Son of God.

> All who rely on observing the law are under a curse, for it is written: "Cursed is everyone who does not continue to do everything written in the Book of the Law." Clearly no one is justified before God by the law, because, "The righteous will live by faith." The law is not based on faith; on the contrary, "The man who does these things will live by them." Christ redeemed us from the curse of the law by becoming a curse for us, for it is written: "Cursed is everyone who is hung on a tree." He redeemed us in order that the blessing given to Abraham might come to the Gentiles through Christ Jesus, so that by faith we might receive the promise of the Spirit. (Gal. 3:10-14)

Paul here distinguishes between two ways of approaching God. One route relies on law and keeping it accurately. The other is based on one's trust in what Jesus has done for his followers.

Paul says that anyone who follows the first approach comes under the curse of his or her inadequacy. He quotes Deuteronomy 27:26 and makes the same point found in James 2:10. Anyone seeking to approach God through keeping law (i.e., any law, whether the Law of Moses, the law written on the heart, or the New Testament understood as law) is doomed to failure. None of us can keep the law of God perfectly, therefore all of us are sinners. Because we are sinners, we are under a curse.

The second approach is through the finished work of Jesus. Knowing that we could not be justified by our efforts at observing law, Jesus came and took the responsibility of our salvation to himself. He set us free from enslavement to law by honoring every command of God and then offering himself as a substitutionary sacrifice for us. He stepped between us and the death blow we were due. Justice was satisfied when sin's penalty—death—was exacted. Mercy was granted when sinners—you and I—were allowed to have that payment credited to our account.

Law says, "Obey, and you shall live." Gospel says, "Believe in what Jesus did, and you shall live." People of law bargain with the Lord and insist that he give them credit for their righteousness. People of faith trust God and allow him to work out his righteousness in them.

Does this mean that Christians are not responsible to law? Does it say that we are exempt from civil, moral, or divine law? Does it mean that we have no obligation to obey men or God? Absolutely not. We embrace, appreciate, and obey law to the best of our ability. But we do not trust our salvation to that. We trust our salvation to Jesus Christ and to him alone.

But look again at the startling language Paul used to explain how Christ accomplished his saving work on our behalf: "Christ redeemed us from the curse of the law by becoming a curse for us" (Gal. 3:13a). Did you catch the play on words? "Christ redeemed us from the curse of the law by becoming a curse for us." How so? "For it is written: 'Cursed is everyone who is hung on a tree'" (Gal. 3:13b; cf. Deut. 21:23).

> *Jesus' cross is not as appealing a sight as his cradle, but it is the more significant of the two.*

Hanging was not a Jewish method of execution. Neither was crucifixion. The hanging of a body referred to in the Old Testament text is probably an allusion to the practice of taking a criminal's body (usually killed by stoning) and impaling him on a stake or nailing him to a tree. It was an act of contempt and utter humiliation. The Law of Moses forbade leaving a body so cursed hanging overnight lest it somehow defile the nation and the land.

Paul took the liberty of using that text to dramatize what happened in the crucifixion of Jesus of Nazareth.

He became a curse for us. He subjected himself to contempt and humiliation for our sakes. He didn't simply die for us. He died a ghastly and offensive death.

Jesus' cross is not as appealing a sight as his cradle, but it is the more significant of the two. It is the event for whose sake the other happened. It is the one we must see in prospect for the other to have its ultimate meaning for us.

When you see gifts beneath your Christmas tree this year, think of God's gift to you. When you see meaningful things such as your children's pictures or the ornaments they made hanging on that tree, remember that God hung on a tree outside Jerusalem. Know that it was done to save you. And please, don't refuse the gift.